Adventures in Sufism

Adventures in Sufism

Stories of a Bronx Childhood

Michael Greenstein

Abandoned Ladder

Adventures in Sufism: Stories of a Bronx Childhood
Copyright © 2012 by Michael Greenstein

Published by Abandoned Ladder
http://www.abandonedladder.com

Except as permitted under U.S. Copyright Law, no part of this book may be reprinted, reproduced, transmitted, or utilized in any form by any electronic, mechanical, or other means, now known or hereafter invented, including photocopying, microfilming, and recording, or in any information storage or retrieval system, without written permission from Michael Greenstein.

Printed in the United States of America

ISBN-13: 978-0615603162 (Abandoned Ladder)
ISBN-10: 0615603165

10 9 8 7 6 5 4 3 2 1

Preface

I began writing this in 1989 for my four year old son when I was diagnosed with cancer. Amid all the fears and uncertainties, I was most concerned that I would fade into his memory. My wife had lost her father when she was two years old, too early for her to have a firm grasp of him. The only piece of him that remained totally hers was a small photograph of herself as a little girl, bundled up in a winter coat, hand outstretched, holding on to him to steady herself.

I didn't want an old photo to be all that I left Nathaniel or Noah, my older son, though I felt as the older of the two, he would somehow carry memories of me intact inside him. I was intrigued by the ending of the movie *Terminator*, where Linda Hamilton's character dictates her story into a tape recorder for her unborn child. With no clear direction, I started writing. I wanted to leave behind an inheritance of memories, especially the development of my spirituality. I wrote about my meetings with Sam, my spiritual teacher, in a series of brief vignettes. These meetings occurred while I was in my early twenties, which was about twenty years before the onset of my illness, but they were turning points in my life and they were a good place to start. But as I progressed in my cancer treatment I wasn't motivated to keep writing.

I completed about 20 pages during my illness and showed them to a few people who gave me encouraging responses. I then asked several other friends to write about their experiences with Sam but only one friend, Stew, did. We self published a little book and called it Servant of God.

But I wasn't satisfied with what I wrote for that publication for a number of reasons:

- I didn't fully explain certain passages. Some needed more detail, others could have benefited by explaining their impact on me at the time.

- I felt uncomfortable writing about certain experiences, fearful that I might cause needless hurt to people while they were still alive.

- Some readers told me that they didn't understand the context or background of the event I was describing.

- I wanted to write for a broader audience. Although some of the events in my life might appear to be unreal to some people, the experiences I describe did happen, and they helped shape who I am. I wanted to share them and introduce people who are interested in developing their spirituality to the possibility of what may be available to them.

- I read many first person accounts of meetings with teachers and gurus. Some were in far away places and far away times. I could not connect on an emotional level with what most authors were trying to impart. I would wolf down these books without really reading them closely, looking for clues to my own spirituality. I didn't find much, but the books themselves held out the hope that something was there to be found. I now know this to be true. I believe you can learn to recognize the important sign posts in your life and follow them.

- I felt that in writing about what I experienced in New York City, I might be able to reach a different audience and add something useful to this literature.

In writing this book, I relied, in part, upon my notes about experiences and records of dreams that I maintained during this period. Several passages were taken directly from my original notes. Other passages flowed directly from my memories. Many names in this book were changed to protect privacy.

— 1 —
Family

Meditation

a large, transparent glass building made up of a maze of interlocking steel beams

each beam is connected to many others and your eye is drawn inward to the core

the building is built entirely around and supports a fragile wooden hut at its center.

Chapter 1. Family

Dad

Dad was very intelligent and self-taught. He had wide-ranging interests, read everything and retained what he read. He left school after the eighth grade and worked at manual labor like many unfortunate children in the 1930s. In one of his early jobs he hauled garbage from dumb waiters, earning him the nickname, "Dusty." He would often tell the story of borrowing a nickel from his mother to buy shopping bags which he would then resell on the subway. His day was made when he made enough to repay her and go the movies, which he didn't leave until closing. My father idolized his mother who worked cleaning other people's floors to bring in food for her family of eight children, but he didn't say much about his father who, when he worked, rolled cigars for a living. Like many people who lived through the depression, poverty formed an indelible imprint on my father's soul.

Dad had four sisters and three brothers. I don't think there ever was a time when he was on speaking terms with all of them at once. I remember when he said the prayer for the dead over one of his sisters, who was very much alive. "If you ever see her on the street," he instructed with his finger a few inches from my face, "pass her by. She is no longer alive to you." Of course, he was on good terms with her a few months later, only to resume another fight weeks after this. His constant battles with his family destroyed any chances I had of bonding with my cousins on his side of the family. One fight that raged the longest among his siblings concerned their mother, who was now senile. Who would take care of her and who would pay for her care? I only have a few memories of my grandmother Becky. During one visit, after her illness had set in, we played a card game, Casino. She cheated and got angry when I pointed it out. Once my father took me to visit her in the hospital but I was not allowed upstairs. I was forced to sit in the car on a cold winter day for an entire afternoon, waiting for his visit to be over. I have even fewer memories of his father, Morris. He had little patience for children and he showed little interest in me.

As a young man dad was romantically involved with a woman from Cleveland. When she became serious, he tried to enlist in the British Foreign Legion to avoid a commitment to her, but he was too young and they rejected him. He later met and married my mother ten weeks after meeting her before leaving to serve in World War II. Some say he was changed man when he came home after the war. Perhaps he internalized much of the fury and rage that is integral to the soldier's experience. However, there is evidence of a cruel streak even in his childhood. His younger brother, already an older man when he talked to me, recounted with vivid detail stories of my father beating him with his fists as a young boy.

After the war, Dad worked many years for a dairy concern. He started off driving a truck and worked his way up to sales representative. He always believed that he should have advanced further in his career but his short temper held him back. During one disagreement, he told off his boss and was fired.

At his best, Dad was fair-minded and had an innate sense of justice and morals. In an old-fashioned way, he was loyal and loving to his family, to his brothers and sisters and to his country. He prided himself on being a good provider to his family and giving his sons the opportunities he did not have. He was psychologically astute with everyone except himself. He also had immense charm, especially to women of all ages. His presence filled up a room. When he passed away following a stroke at the age of 78 I felt a major shift in the universe, as a force in the world had departed.

The key to my survival was keeping away from him. My life revolved around knowing his plans, when he was getting home from work, and especially what time he would eat meals. Whenever possible I ate dinner before he arrived home from work and stayed in my room, out of his

Chapter 1. Family

sight. When he was home, I would address any questions or needs I might have to my mother or brother when he was out of earshot, so that he would have less of an opportunity to overhear my conversation and ridicule or demean me. TV time, when the family would gather around the small black and white Philco, and weekends were always points of vulnerability. We were once watching a ball game on TV (the New York Giants, of course) and my father said to me, "Look, he hit the ball down the second base line." I knew I was in for trouble but was filled with fear and indecision. Why did he say such an idiotic thing? What did he want me to do? Correcting him was out of the question. I said nothing, waiting for a clue about how to proceed, but guessed wrong. Whack. The heel of his hand smashed against the side of my head. "I knew you were stupid," he muttered. "How could you not know there is no second base line?" I said nothing, waiting for the pain to subside, this time guessing correctly. If I showed fear, or moved, or cried, he could be pushed over the edge. Mostly, it would be the screaming. The in-your-face, top of the lungs, vein bulging in the forehead variety. I had a strict credo that I would follow whenever I had to interact with my dad: Stand tall. Don't move. Show no emotion.

If I was lucky, he wouldn't hit me again, just continue with the verbal barrage. "You'll amount to nothing, a nobody. What do they teach you in school?" he continued. And then in a calm, almost plaintive voice, "How can you be so stupid?" At this point, I knew I survived to face another day. But there was always more to endure. The second half to every misery was his recounting of events to whoever was available: my mother, my brother, visiting aunts and uncles. This was a second source of danger. I dare not contradict him or retell events from my perspective. While he would not hit me in front of an audience, I would not be spared from his verbal wrath. His excesses were all too obvious. It was a small measure of comfort to hear his sister refer to him as "Crazy Joey" or to have others try to comfort me saying, "You know how he is..." I knew only too well. Grandma, exasperated with his bullying, had even called him "Hitler" on a few occasions, this being the worst epithet she could muster. Surprisingly, this had a salutary effect as it amused him. He would retell this story many times as a sign of her weakness.

If you challenged him, he might tell you that it was none of your business. He would say that he knew what he wanted for his sons and that no one was going to interfere with his right to raise us the way he wanted. And that's just about how it went. It wasn't only his words that would cause a person to back off but the accompanying physical response: the raised tone of voice, the narrowing of the eyes, the utmost seriousness of expression. These were signs of impending danger, not just to me but to everyone else as well. You didn't want to mess with a guy who could suddenly transform himself into a concentrated point of fury. A guy wound so tight that one perceived transgression would cause him to pounce. And pounce he did. Anyone who had a choice would back away. My mother and I were not so lucky. Our lives in the early days were molded simply by our reactions to him.

I was not very sensitive to nuance, took matters too literally, and didn't always understand things well the first time I heard them. This often put me at odds with my father, whose communications seemed to carry several meanings. "Get me that over there," he would say in conversational voice, without looking up from his chair. I would look at the table, see his Pall Malls, his lighter, an ashtray, the newspaper, maybe a bowl of fruit. What exactly is "over there?" I would quickly gather myself together and go over my learned list of questions that I could execute at lightning speed:

> What is the context of this question?
> Note the tone of voice: how near was he to losing control?

Chapter 1. Family

Did he expect me to answer? Or was he being rhetorical?
Did he expect me to do something?
Did I understand the instructions? Do I risk bringing over the wrong thing or do I ask him for clarification?
Which is least likely to get me in trouble?
Was anyone else present who could silently point me in the right direction?

If he got unhinged, show no fear. And, always listen to the words. There is an instruction that I must follow. If I guessed right, I would escape with only this momentary anxiety. If I guessed wrong, he might simply tell me what he wanted or I might risk anything from a quick slap to another round of verbal humiliation.

One hot summer day, tired of reading books and not knowing what to do, I came to my mother and told her I was bored. This was a major goof. My father came bounding from the other room. "Bored," he screamed, "You're not going to be bored anymore. You will memorize the dictionary. Five words a day and I'm going to test you when I come home from work and God help you if you don't know them." My first thought was, "Is he serious?" But I knew better. On the following evening we never got to the words and their definitions. There was a smudge on the corner of the paper I used which acted like tinder to my father's sensibilities. "Is this how you hand in work at school, with smudges?" The decibel level was so loud I was sure that all my old teachers, wherever they might be, were listening. "Your work must be perfect," he insisted. He wouldn't look at the list and returned it to me in disdain. Now I had a small dilemma. Were 10 words due on the next day, or only the revision to the first five on Day 1? I prepared two lists of five words each on separate pages and gave him the first list. He gave it a glancing look but instead of testing me from the list, he went straight to the dictionary. The words on my list were not the same as in the dictionary. "What is going on?" he demanded. I had not anticipated this. I had skipped abbreviations, interjections, words I knew, two letter words. Some words had multiple meanings and I only wrote down the first one. He actually listened to me then, settled down and accepted my response. As the summer was coming to an end and the school term beginning, he relieved me from this project. But for years he would remind me of the lasting "benefits" of this assignment and, as an example, pointed out that I learned how to spell the word "aardvark." This is the first time I ever used that word in a sentence, but he was very proud of what he believed he accomplished.

A few weeks later my father took me and my young twin cousins Mona and Marcy to the Bronx Zoo. When he wasn't looking, my cousins threw every imaginable piece of garbage at the animals. Not wanting to be outdone in these exploits, and having nothing to throw, I tried to spit at a bear but only managed to dribble spittle down the front of my jacket. "I spit at the bear," I exclaimed to my cousins in triumph. The problems was, my father overheard. I was sure he knew that I wasn't the only guilty party, but he wasn't concerned about the actions of my cousins. He had paid little attention to them. He took me aside and said in a low voice that when we got home I was to remind him about this so he could wash my mouth out with soap. I was stunned. I had to remind him! Well, I was determined to forget. Maybe he would get distracted and forget too. I was silently grateful for the presence of my cousins. Although their mischief prompted me to act, their very presence saved me from an immediate beating. When the trip was over and the day was winding down I was watching a TV show hoping my father had forgotten about his threatened punishment. No such luck."Have you forgot to remind me that you had your punishment coming" he asked sarcastically. "I forgot" I stammered. "You forgot" he said, with even more sarcasm. He grabbed

Chapter 1. Family

me by the back of my neck and half dragged me into the bathroom. Pinning my body against the sink he forced my mouth open and shoved in a bar of soap as far as he could, causing me to gag. He then twisted the bar in my mouth with such force that I thought my teeth would break. He continued to scrape the bar against my teeth with senseless fury. He then left me in tears, my mother screaming when she saw what he had done.

One day when I as about 13, something different happened. I don't remember the circumstances but I do remember the raised hand inching closer to my face when, like a boxer, bobbing and weaving, I leaned back in self defense, away from the blow. I timed it perfectly. He missed me completely. But the suddenness of the move put me off balance. Involuntarily, I took a few steps back on my heels trying to regain my equilibrium and more importantly, my poise, but I fell down, humiliated and in great fear as to what fury I was about to unleash. But he just laughed. He hadn't even touched me, and there I was sprawled on my back. "Look at the way you bounced," he giggled. "That's it, 'Bouncer,' that's what I'll call you."

A new phase in our relationship began. The lectures, already long, became longer. I had to maintain my serious mien, look him directly in the eye and take my berating. It wasn't over until the tears welled up in my eyes. He would sum up his indictment, sickened by another sign of my weakness until by chance, I stumbled across a way to maintain my self-control. In the middle of one of his tirades I felt my composure slipping. Coincidentally, I noticed a large smudge on my glasses and took them off to give them a wipe around with my hanky. Immediately, there was a measure of relief. I could look at something other than his face, to do something other than drink in the words of disappointment. His image became a blurry fuzz in my near-sighted glory. His words seemed to be floating in air, directed towards no one, a haze of anger I could dissociate from. I was now able to sit through these sessions, regain self control and slowly begin the process of engaging him in conversation without succumbing to mind-numbing fear.

Dad's habit of taking offense at the slightest provocation was not limited to his immediate family. Heaven help anyone who tried to take a parking spot away from him. Once a guy raced him for a spot but lost out near the 167th Street Cafeteria in the Bronx. My father saw him later in the day eating an ice cream and this poor soul made the mistake of smirking in the direction of my father. It didn't make a difference that he was younger and bigger, dad took his ice cream and threw it in his face. My mother got into the act and began hitting the guy with her pocketbook. I rolled over in laughter.

One day when I was in 10th grade Dad asked me what I had for homework. I told him not much, that I had to define some terms for biology. He asked to see the list and noted that I had no definition for endoplasmic reticulum. "It wasn't in my textbook," I explained. "And you left it at that," he asked unbelievingly. "We're going to find it," he said matter-of-factly. And we searched every super market dictionary and encyclopedia in the house but nothing revealed the inner workings of this cell structure. So after what seemed like hours my father pieced together a definition of the words from their roots and came pretty close to what the teacher expected. Although he could not leave well enough alone and chastised me for giving up so soon, I reluctantly enjoyed the process of discovery. The hardest part about these tasks was that I never knew when to expect them. They were seemingly random, yet my father had an intuitive quality that allowed him to strike at the worst time.

I have an old photo of my father. He is about 18 years old but in this picture he looks older. He is sporting a moustache and wearing a tie, top coat and a stylish hat. All the features are fuzzy as if the photo is underdeveloped. His lips are parted but he is not quite smiling. It is hard to figure out what he is thinking. He seems full of undeveloped potential, as he seemed all his life.

Mom

After my parents married my father was away at war in Europe for almost four years. He came back shell-shocked and for all practical purposes, was not the man my mother married. Mom's parents told her to divorce, that they would support her and baby Allen, but she wouldn't hear of it. My father's personality, which was always strong, was now a force of nature. When he had his mind set on something he was immovable and persistent. He pressed his will with a relentless energy. He bulldozed my mother until her self esteem tumbled. She could not escape this steady, natural force of nature wearing her down, telling her what to think and what to do. Over time she learned it was easier to give in and accept a passive role, at least in front of him. Even as a child I noticed how different she was, how alive, with other people. In my father's presence she remained feisty, but the light in her eyes continued to dim. Something in her seemed missing, as if you only saw her shadow.

The center of my mother's life was her children. She loved and protected my brother and me with all the fierceness in her spirit. She became overprotective, especially with me, watching over me when I walked to school or played outside even though I was old enough to be more independent. When I was quite young, she taught me to pray and each night we would recite the poem, "Now I lay me down to sleep." I never thought much about what the words meant, but I felt a closeness and connection to God developing from an early age. Over time, this connection began to slip away from me as conflicting messages about God, my own budding spirituality and the drudgery of Hebrew school failed to make any sense to me or provide me with any source of peace.

When I was nine, my mother miscarried. I was shocked that I did not even know she was pregnant. The possibility of having another brother or sister left me dazed. I remember my father being very tender to my mother but she was inconsolable. In the wake of this disaster the course of her life changed. She became an alcoholic and drank for the next thirteen years. She also lost faith in God, for how could God let this happen to her? Everyone who was close to my mother has stories about her drinking. At first, she drank too much at family gatherings and my brother would carry her back home. Later on, she drank late at night from bottles she hid around the house. She would hide booze in apple juice bottles, vegetable oil bottles, unmarked glass bottles next to the cleaning supplies, her underwear drawer and at the bottom of the clothes hamper in the bathroom. Most Friday nights I would find her passed out on the couch, with a lit cigarette in her hand, and I would put her to bed As with many things, my father was the last to know.

My mother's drinking was both an outward sign of her deep feelings of despair, but it was also a defiant act of rebellion. It achieved a source of payback as it clearly drove my father crazy. Yet, it was another trigger for his yelling and his lectures and this perpetrated the cycle. When I was sixteen, dad came up with an act of desperation that I thought was ingenious. He suggested that we take in a foster child. Mom, he knew, would fall in love with a child and he felt that it might focus her attention and energies in a positive direction. He was partially right. Mom never drank during the day, waiting for Max to fall asleep before guzzling her stash. Maxie, as he was introduced to us, stayed with us for about a year. A shy child, behind in his school, he became more outgoing and academically focused as he began to settle down. He was just beginning to flourish and made some friends when his father and new wife suddenly appeared from nowhere and asked the social service agency for him back. It was hard on all of

Chapter 1. Family

us. We were all shocked when his father greeted him and called him Scott. We never knew that was his first name. I visited Scott a couple of times at his parent's house. Scott seemed angry, arrogant and was messing up in school. My visits took place in their small, drab kitchen. I hardly had any time alone with Scott. No one seemed to be having much fun. I stopped calling and never saw Scott again.

Of all my mother's endearing qualities, cooking was not one of them. She would make chicken soup every Friday night and then took that same chicken and broiled it until its skin resembled shoe leather. It was so dry and tasteless, I can think of no apt comparison. But that was the way my father liked it, so that was the way it was served. To avoid the inevitable conflict with my father, I began sitting down to Friday night dinner at 4 PM. I would sit and complain for a good 90 minutes, begging to eat anything else or bargaining on portion size. I tried every condiment in my house: salt, pepper, garlic powder, ketchup and three kinds of mustard: French's, Gulden's and Chinese but nothing would help. As if following an unwritten script, the drama always came to a quick close long before my father came home from work. I always had to eat some portion of the tasteless chicken, but not before I used every stratagem I could think of to minimize the damage. My most effective method was to stuff the chicken in napkins, hide them in my pocket and flush the evidence away. Sometimes I took a more direct approach, hiding the pieces at the bottom of the garbage or tossing them out the third story window.

Mom excelled at bargain hunting and never let a sale go unnoticed. She would never buy just one when two could be claimed at a discount and Alexander's on Fordham Road became a second home to me. She was sharp with figures and even sharper at negotiating the best price. It didn't make a difference if it was the kosher butcher, the Fuller Brush man or the seltzer man. Those extra pennies went into her secret stash and quickly turned into dollars.

Years later, when my parents moved, my father counted 80 boxes of canned goods. My father asked her, "Where are the savings? How much tuna fish can you eat in a lifetime? We're giving it all back to the moving men! " But it was too late to change old habits.

If there was something Mom did better than save, it was playing Gin Rummy. You might win a game or two, but in the long run, if you played her for money, you were going down.

My brother was obviously my father's favorite and I, needy and vulnerable, drifted into my mother's sphere. Both of us needed acceptance and nurturing and our needs bonded us in mutual dependence. While the demons related to interactions with my father were clear and obvious to me, the negative effects of my dependent relationship with my mother were subtle and below the level of my awareness for many years.

I have a photo of my mother holding me as a baby. I was the prettiest baby with blond curls and a delicious smile. I am being held in my mother's strong arms in the street, outside our apartment. The photo captures the blur of me clapping my hands in excitement as the expression on my mother's face is the look of a woman who loves her child more than life itself.

Allen

Five years older and 6 years ahead of me in school, my brother Allen was not only stronger and wiser as only a big brother can be, but he was also the best and the brightest to most who knew him. He had charismatic qualities that attracted people of all ages. He was a natural center of attention throughout my childhood and I loved him and admired him as my hero. He helped me with my homework, took me on trips to Madison Square Garden to see rodeos and the hapless NY Knicks, taught me to play ball, shared the inside knowledge of living in our household and

Chapter 1. Family

tried to teach me survival skills. We played marbles on our linoleum floor for hours. I wasn't wrong or stupid, or even smart or talented when I was with him. I was just a kid, his younger brother. He gave me a sense of normalcy that I didn't have anywhere else.

Allen was the architect of one of my favorite childhood days. He took me to the movies to see a Tarzan adventure, then we went to another movie to see the first James Bond adventure, Dr. No. After this we went to eat Chinese food, pizza and to top it off, egg creams.

Accomplished as much in school as on the street, I lived and breathed vicariously through his many achievements. I felt bonded to him as if his very existence kept me alive. It did. The happiness I recall from my childhood years is intimately connected to my brother's experiences. He taught me by example and most important of all, he was the only one in the family who could survive in my father's presence. When I was young, I used to think that he was immune from my father's wrath, but as I later learned, this was not so. Allen got a healthy start by being doted on for three years by my mother, her mother and two sisters while my father was off to war in Europe. When dad came back to see the son he never met, Allen got the brunt of my father's impatience and anger. Allen may have gotten lucky when my father hit him so hard that he punctured his eardrum. It was a blessing in disguise. He never hit him again. After that dad turned his attention to more vulnerable targets. Allen was also adept at finding ways around our father. He could give the appearance of doing what my father wanted while doing what he pleased when the situation permitted. If I had learned this skill, I would have been much better off, but my constitution was different and I took my fathers criticisms to heart.

Grandma

My mother's monther, Grandma Brucha was only 67 when she died. Young by today's standards, yet she was always the same age to me: old. One of my earliest childhood memories is of her. I was sleeping in her bed, clinging to my bottle. I woke up, unscrewed the cap and poured the milk over her. She awoke with a start, looked at me and laughed. "Why tatala, why did you do such a thing?" she asked in her unmistakable East-European Yiddish voice. "I wanted to give you a bath," I replied. She laughed again, louder this time, and got up to change the linen.

She told me about her life in Europe although I don't remember much. I was too young to appreciate such stories and the thoughts of losing her family during the war always brought tears to her eyes. Her father had property and some farm animals but earned his wage making coats for the soldiers in the Czar's army. She was very proud that he was able to provide tutors for her so she received a proper education as a young girl. I made her tell me over and over again about when she traveled across Russia with mother and brother to meet Rasputin. Her brother fell or got sick and was unable to use his leg. I have no idea how they traveled or how long the journey took but they eventually appeared before the towering man who had flames in his eyes. "Walk," he commanded, extending his hand and fingers towards the boy. And walk he did. I think she was afraid of that giant until the day she died. This story, and the possibilities it suggested about human capacity, fascinated me.

Passover Seders at her house are forever inscribed as some of the happiest memories of my childhood. We would all dress up and gather at her apartment along with my mothers' sisters and their families. The kitchen table and a folding table would be set up in the living room for the 18 of us. It was so magnificent with fine linens, china and silverware. The air was charged with excitement and

Chapter 1. Family

I especially enjoyed the company of my younger cousins. My father led the Seder in English and we all pitched in, reading from Hagadahs that came in the mail from organizations seeking donations or were freebies distributed to liquor stores. They were carefully preserved from Seder to Seder. Their wine stained pages and creased covers seemed to give these pamphlets dignity for having survived the rigors of so many Seders.

I was allowed to drink the sickly sweet Manischewitz grape wine and developed quite a fondness for it over the years. My whole meal could have consisted of matzo balls and choroset, but of course, there was a lot more. After the meal was eaten, the three sisters disappeared to clean up the dishes and chat among themselves while the men continued with the service. I dreaded the prospect of being the youngest child with facility in Hebrew and having to sing the Four Questions. I had a terrific command of Hebrew, so I wasn't worried about making a mistake but I was anxious about the idea of everyone looking at me. I always did a good job and eventually, to my great relief, everyone sang together.

There was a section of the text that took on growing significance to me. The rabbis ask us not just to retell the story and say to the prayers but to imagine that it was "we," the present day readers of the Hagadah, who were freed from bondage. When I was young this passage gave me a sense of connection to my Jewish heritage and also to present day Jews who I saw, in my mind's eye, as reading the same words at the same time in their own homes. When I got older I began to think of all the ways I was still a slave in the world: a slave to desire, to greed, to the opinions of others. Where was my Moses to lead me to my salvation?

As my grandmother got older, the scene shifted to my Aunt Dotty's house in New Jersey. Life in this quiet suburban community could not be more different than the tenement walk-up in the Bronx. Most of the cooking genes in the family were inherited by Aunt Dotty and she outdid herself with graciousness and love each year. As her luck would have it, she would always get the part of the Hagadah to read with either long Hebrew names or the single reference to "breasts" in the text. Both would render her silly and the whole table would join her in laughter.

Grandma read me stories from the Jewish newspaper, the *FORWARD*, and sang Yiddish songs that I could not comprehend. When I was a teenager, Grandma stayed with us for a while after suffering a heart attack. This was some time after husband #2 and before #3. My father, in an act of generosity, asked if it would be ok with me for grandma to stay with us. This being a euphemism for sharing my bedroom. It would have been perfectly acceptable for him if I said no. Perhaps he counted on it. But I said yes readily. I didn't know what I would be getting into but I knew from the depth of my feelings for her, and her needs, that I had no real choice in the matter. Once some questions are asked, there is only one proper response. Besides, if she needed someone to look after her, there was no better caretaker than my mother. I instantly forged two secret hopes. One was that another person in the house might provide a calming influence on my father. The other was that Grandma's presence might put a dent in my mother's drinking. I was wrong on both counts. As grandma got stronger, her feistiness returned. She had a knack, like few people did, of pushing every one of my father's buttons. Instead of calming things down a bit, there were now more opportunities for personal interaction with my father to go wrong. Grandma also witnessed, first hand, the effects of my mother's drinking and was powerless to stop it. After she regained her health, she moved back into her own apartment and married husband #3, a cousin from the old country. I was honored to be the best man at her wedding.

One of the casualties of Grandma moving in with us was the loss of my personal space. Bottles of perfume

Chapter 1. Family

and lots of old lady things occupied the tops of what once was my dresser and desk. They all went with her when she moved out with the exception of a round vanity mirror, which she used to apply heavy doses of rouge, powders and creams. It had a regular mirror on one side and a magnifying mirror on the other that was particularly unkind. When she wasn't using it, it doubled as my zit-picking mirror. I don't know why she left it behind, but years later, this mirror revealed to me some very hard truths.

Grandma had some nice jewelry. Nothing to make Harry Winston jealous, but before she got sick and died, she gave it all to her youngest daughter for safe keeping. The reason she did this is part of family mythology. Some say she did not want it to fall into the hands of her third husband's children. Other reasons were that she was afraid that my mother might drink it all away or that her other daughter, Dotty, didn't need it. Perhaps all the reasons were true. But when she died, Chandie, the youngest and neediest daughter, told her sisters that Grandma had given it all to her. And she kept it. She offered no explanation and this caused a rift between the sisters that lasted more than a decade. I lost contact with two of my close cousins, similar to what I had experienced with my father's family. When I was in my twenties and on my own, I gave my aunt a call one day and went over for dinner. My mother, angry and disappointed for years, was by this time looking for an excuse to get back with her sister. My visit began the slow thaw.

My mother took Grandma's prized pots, cast iron pans and some exquisite silver and copper serving pieces that I took from her and have to this day. I also rescued from the garbage my grandmother's old Persian carpet that had many worn and frayed spots. I have been using this carpet ever since.

— 2 —
Into The World

Dream

I am on the roof of the building where I grew up.
It is a clear summer evening. I don't know what I'm doing there.
I look around.
Standing about 20 feet away is the Devil, shrouded in black. I do not have time to react. He extends his arm towards me and upwards and suddenly I am raised high off the ground. I am petrified. He sweeps his arm to the left and suspends me over the side of the building. The great height, the Devil and my impending doom bring me to near panic and I know that I will be smashed down to the pavement below.
But I become aware that I am protected as if inside an unbreakable bubble. I know no harm will come to me.

Chapter 2. Into The World

760

The four of us, my parents, my brother, and I lived in a three bedroom apartment on the third floor at 760 East 178th Street. The apartment number was 4C which confused people who came to visit us for the first time. They naturally assumed that the apartment was on the fourth floor, but that's not the way the building was designed. The first floor had the "A" apartments, the second, the "B" apartments, and so on. There was a long hallway leading from the apartment door. A bedroom was on the immediate right. Then down 10 feet or so was the bathroom and down another 10 feet was the kitchen, the living room and two bedrooms off the living room. The building had been built in the 1880's, had a dumbwaiter for garbage, high ceilings, and had decorative moldings around the ceiling. The bedrooms were large and airy.

We had a small fish tank with fresh water fish and a bookcase with old dusty books in the middle of the hallway. It was on this bookcase that I found She and a dozen other books by H. Rider Haggard when I was old enough to read. He was to become one of my favorite authors as books would be a constant source of comfort and learning for me.

The window from the kitchen faced out onto the street. Everything about our world that needed to be seen could be spied from that perch. My mother would sit by the window and take her position, leaning on her elbows. The street where the boys played stickball, the corner to Prospect Avenue, the street leading up to the public school and down to the Hebrew school was all within her watchfulness.

I was comfortable with the routines of the house. We ate dairy on Tuesdays, spaghetti on Thursdays, and chicken on Friday night. My mother kept a kosher home and had duplicate sets of everything for the meat and diary dishes. Although I did not realize it at the time, the house was spotless, our clothes were spotless and my mother made sure that I was "spotless" and clean, too. The center of the living room was taken by the big Philco TV which in later years gave way to the Zenith. Unattractive linoleum covered the floors. There were no pictures on the walls and no priceless art treasures from school found their way onto the clean, white refrigerator. Only a few photographs were displayed: my parents wedding picture in their bedroom and a few posed pictures of Allen and me when were little in the long hallway.

I had a sense of stability. Tremont Avenue, the main shopping fare, remained relatively intact throughout my growing up years. We went to the same bakery, pharmacy, dry cleaning store, Chinese restaurant, pizza place, supermarket, candy store and movie houses without variation. I knew my public school, where I would go to Junior High School, High School and college (nothing other than the free city colleges was an option.). The streets were always dangerous and to hear my parents talk, the neighborhood was always changing for the worse. My parents, my brother, my grandmother, my aunts and uncles, and even neighbors were, for the most part, an active presence in my life.

Yet with all this support, it wasn't enough to sustain my mental health so that I could have what most would call a "normal" childhood. My father's vision of who I was, weak, lazy and stupid, became my own. I harbored a secret despondency. I was not suicidal. Killing myself would have been too assertive and too repulsive an act. I was capable of a certain amount of planning and was a master of avoidance, but the notion of purposeful self destruction was foreign to me. What I wanted, in the most unspeakable part of me, was for the pain to stop. My self esteem was non-existent. Self loathing was the background noise of my life, the ever present constant, the medium through which I experienced myself: My unwished-for wish was to be dead.

Chapter 2. Into The World

Bully

With self-awareness of my own despair and helplessness, I could easily diagnose frailty in others and find kids who could be victims to my bullying. The earliest target for my silent, quiet fury was a boy named Stephen. I began getting into fights with him and beating him up in second grade. I didn't like him much, I could take him - that was reason enough.

There are some moments in life that have pristine clarity. There is a quiet perfection to them, like watching a scene in a movie which has suddenly, silently, switched to slow-motion. Nothing else exists but the characters in that scene. One such moment occurred a couple of years later on a snowy day when I was walking home from Hebrew school. I spotted a small child playing in the snow across the street between parked cars. I put down my school books, took off my gloves and dug my hands into the snow. I made the perfect "snow baseball" and I threw the perfect line drive pitch. I saw it sail silently across the street guided by some invisible navigation system. It seemed to be gathering force as it landed squarely on his forehead, knocking him over into the snow. I was exhilarated. In those brief few seconds I had wordlessly brought together planning, skill, attention to detail and execution and achieved perfect results.

Then he began to cry and the still beauty of the moment shattered. I was filled with horror for I understood, perhaps for the first time, that I was a person in the world responsible for my actions. I saw the connection between the act of forming my missile and throwing it, and the boy's pain and distress. This awareness was self-evident and needed no further examination or thought. Where had this awareness been just a few moments before? I stood there dumbfounded, humiliated and shamed, but too lost in self absorption to think about the crying child. I began to feel that I did a horrible thing but regained my senses when the boy's mother appeared from nowhere and started running towards me. I quickly put on some speed and she retreated to her crying son.

When I was thirteen, I beat up a kid so badly his mother took him to the hospital. She called home to speak to my father. I was petrified, but the upset mother stepped over some imaginary line with him, probably saying that she would send my father the doctor bill. When he told her to stick the phone up her ass I knew I had survived a close call. When he hung up the phone, he asked me calmly what the kid did to deserve this. Seeing my opening, I made up something up to justify my actions and the matter dropped.

In high school I began writing creative assignments in English class. Many of my essays contained similar themes: sad, depressing landscapes that were ravaged by nature. One day, Mr. Lee asked me to read my essay aloud. When I was finished, he asked me, in front of all the students, whether I really felt that way. Embarrassed and flustered, I replied that I was only trying to be creative. I never wrote so revealingly again in class and Mr. Lee never again asked how I felt.

Despite my youthful epiphany, I did not stop my bullying tactics until I was in my early twenties. I should have grown out of this behavior as I got older, but I didn't. I picked on a big, gentle guy named Gerald that I knew from work. I was merciless with my teasing and he should have clocked me. My skills at finding personal weakness were quite honed by this time. I never examined my behavior until one day, in passing, he mentioned that his therapist said something to him about how I needed treatment. This seemingly innocuous statement pierced my defenses. I heard him clearly and his words staggered me. For a moment I was back in that snowy street watching the little boy cry out in pain and surprise. I felt a crack develop in the fragile sense I had of myself as a kind and caring person. Like the snowball incident years before, I had separated the person I thought myself to be from the person who acted so outwardly mean. Although I couldn't tell him, I took his comment to heart and began to connect with a different, healthier side of me. I never picked on Gerald again.

Hebrew School

My parents sent me to Hebrew school when I was ten. It was one of two orthodox shuls within two blocks of my house. I soon learned that this was a very different type of school. For starters, most of the kids in my first grade class were of different ages, the youngest about eight. But it didn't seem to matter. We were all bound together by a common prayer: that the messiah should come and deliver us from this wretched school. No one wanted to be there. And the boys also shared the dreaded purpose behind it all, the Bar Mitzvah, where we would be called to the pulpit in front of a huge group of congregants and family members to solemnly entertain by singing Hebrew prayers in unfamiliar melodies. The major reason I started later than the others was cost. My parents delayed my enrollment until the last possible moment. Each month I had to bring in an envelope to the old men who sat in a dilapidated office. They wouldn't let you just pay and go, they made you wait around and hold the envelope in your hand while they brought out these huge ledger books. Finding your name among the many in the ledger books was their major occupation. Then they studied our payment history and shook their heads slowly from side to side as they grumbled about how little we were paying. These men threatened, insinuated, ignored, humiliated; no tactic was beneath them. At first I was terrified of them. But for the most part I remained quiet. Although I told them that I would tell my parents that we owed them more money, I knew that if they were really serious, they wouldn't be talking to me. So, I silently refused to become their messenger of intimidation to my parents.

The shul was maintained by a non-Jewish couple that got to live in an apartment rent free. The apartment was close to the classrooms and we often saw the woman of the house who performed housekeeping chores. It always amused me to smell the goyish aromas coming from her kitchen. As students we were an untidy lot and threw our candy wrappers and other unwanted stuff in the hallways and in the foyer, where we hung out before and after classes. She made the mistake of asking us not to throw so many things on the floor and we never let up after that. One day someone brought water balloons to school and this infuriated her. When she had her backed turned to us, I took a balloon, put it on my crotch, and walked behind her with a swagger, to the hilarious whoops of the onlookers. With eyes in back of her head, she turned quickly, took me firmly by the arm and marched me downstairs to the office. I was scared, not from anything the woman or the men in the office might do, but because there was the possibility of a call home leading to more wrath from my father. We waited in silence. The woman was exasperated and agitated. And suddenly I saw her problem. What was she going to say to these old men? We were ushered into the holy sanctum and she sputtered and fumbled over her words. Finally, she said that she couldn't tell them what I did, for she was a gentlewoman and left me there to explain. When her footsteps died, the oldest of the old men asked me what happened. I took a moment to realize the new position I was in. "Nothing," I said matter-of-factly.

"Nothing" an incredulous voice asked. "She brought you here for nothing?"

"Nothing," I said, trying to keep my voice steady. "Who are you going to believe, me or this Shiksa?" I said with derision. The old men looked at each other and I was excused.

In my first two years of Hebrew School my teacher was Mrs. Bitter, a woman who was pre-programmed to love me because I was the brother of her beloved Allen. I became a star in my own right and after two years, skipped three grades and was put in a class of boys my own age. But to my surprise I came to find out that this distinction had only happened once before in the history of our school. But there was an ulterior motive behind the teachers' thinking. If there was a possibility that I might want to go to Hebrew High School, I needed to be in a class with boys my own age. Despite the big jump, I held my own in class which was conducted mostly in Hebrew. But I hated it. The teacher was a strict disciplinarian and he didn't care for the kids. The classroom was not air conditioned and all the good kids sat in the first rows to be near the teacher. In the late spring, the room became a sauna. I sat alone, in the back, near the big windows to catch a breeze. One day when I was looking out at the window, Mr. A. caught me. This was his big moment. He continued talking but made his way to the back of the class until he stood in front of me. I knew I was caught but wouldn't give him the satisfaction of returning my gaze and admitting defeat.

"What are you looking at?" he screamed at me. I turned slowly.

"It's a beautiful day. The sun is shining, the birds are singing," I replied.

"Perhaps you want to join them?" he bellowed.

"All right," I said, picking up my belongings. I left the room and never came back. My Bar Mitzvah was only a few weeks away. There was nothing he could do.

Little Women

I met Renee when I was 6. She was in my kindergarten class. Renee was warm, caring and sensitive. Quiet but alert. Not very cute, but I didn't care. She was my buddy. We sat together, talked, joked and enjoyed each other's company. This was innocence. Neither of us wanted anything from the other. Then she stopped coming to school.

I wasn't aware of this at first but recognized the emptiness inside me. She was sick and the way Mrs. Schwartz talked, I didn't think she was coming back. The class made get well cards and I was asked to deliver them. My mother walked me over to her apartment building and I met Renee and her mom. Renee was in her pajamas. I recognized the intimacy of this moment but she was as natural and carefree as she was in school. We played together in her room as our mothers talked over coffee. Renee came back to school for only a short while. One day her mother came over to me after kindergarten and told me that they had bought a house and were moving. I was stunned. I had just gotten her back and she was leaving for good. I felt that a piece of me was being ripped out. When we played together there was no thought of past, present or future. Now I felt her loss. I wanted to cry in disbelief but didn't. Renee and I said our goodbyes and we never saw each other again.

Sue lived in the same building as us on the second floor. Our families were friends and we got together with them occasionally. Sue was a year older and we played infrequently. I enjoyed board games, but she favored activities that mimicked domestic life. She especially enjoyed making believe that we were grown ups. This went on for a few years and was quite innocent until one day, when we were about 10, she asked me to play doctor and to examine her. I didn't want to, but she began to take her clothes off. I was petrified and fascinated as she guided my hand to her breast and then to her vagina. I got hard and then she took my pants off to examine me. I was really scared and tried to stop her but the thought of running out of her room and getting caught by her mother was out of the question. Then she mounted me, pushing me inside her. "This is how mommies and daddies make babies" she explained. I felt confused as I didn't know what was going on. I felt embarrassed about being naked, humiliated by her aggressiveness and my passivity and fearful that we

Chapter 2. Into The World

might actually have a baby. I avoided Sue after this and was never alone with her again.

I met Harriet in Hebrew school when I was about 8. I fell in love with her at first sight. She had a model's oval face with large brown eyes and long lashes. Her smile was wide and magnetic. Her brown hair was long and shoulder length. Harriet's beauty, even at this tender age, was astounding and gave me my first taste of undefined longing. I needed to possess her, as if my completeness and acceptance resided within her. I never told Harriet I liked her and wanted her to be my girlfriend but went out of my way to look for her any chance I could and engage her in conversation. This went on for five painfully shy years. Over time, Harriet could not help but notice my interest in her and I began to see a subtle change in the way she responded to me. She was in familiar territory by this time and had lots of male attention. She was waiting for me to make some overture towards her and I didn't think she would reject me. But I was locked in fear. After my Bar Mitzvah I stopped attending Hebrew School and didn't see Harriet again until I bumped into her on the street many years later as a young adult.

Thocolate

Mr. and Mrs. Friedman owned a candy store around the corner of our building. They had a wonderful comic book display but kids weren't allowed to look at them if we weren't buying. I loved Batman, Superman and Green Lantern but my brother turned me on to the joys of Mad Magazine. Mr. Friedman was a grouch, didn't like kids very much and resented making his money by having to do business with them. I liked to order lime rickies when I could afford them, or ice cream sodas, just to make him work. The Mrs. seemed kindly but one day she began some ribbing at my expense. "Thocolate? You want thocolate ice cream?" She said with a touch of sarcasm. It didn't take much to knock me off center. "Isn't anyone telling you to pronounce your words properly?" But no one was. After this incident if I was with my mother or anyone else in the store I would have them order my ice cream for me. If I was alone and had to order for myself, I would get vanilla to avoid embarrassment.

It didn't take the school system long to catch up to me. Speech Defect. DE-FECT, that's what they called it and that's what I thought of myself. This was another blow to my almost non-existent self-esteem. They put me in speech class in the first grade. Little did I know that it would be a life sentence without parole. It was an educational experience of many kinds. Not only did I learn to say "ch" instead of th," I began a lifelong battle to sound like a snake, and conquer my word nemesis: "rail-road." The speech teacher would spend a few minutes with each kid telling us to put our tongues in what seemed to be ridiculous places. Who could talk like that? I was to learn, eventually, most people could.

Speech class lasted about an hour, and when I returned to class I also learned that I didn't need to be present to catch up with what I had missed. As I got older I was also introduced to the politics of itinerant teachers who needed a requisite number of students to justify a school visit and a payday. By the time I reached the 8th grade my speech was certainly intelligible. But I was aware there were many other students who needed this service more than I did. I reached my limit for humiliation, walked out and never returned.

Reading

My best friend was my brother. As youngsters we would shoot marbles across our bedroom floors and down the long hallway in our apartment or spy at girls getting undressed in their apartments across the street with his telescope. But being older and popular, he was often out and

Chapter 2. Into The World

about while I was alone in the house. Summers were particularly brutal and lonely. I was allowed to play in front of the house but not allowed to go into the street to play stick ball or punch ball. To my mother, the street always seemed too dangerous and I, too young. The only kids that hung around the sidewalk were girls and toddlers and I didn't want to hang out with them. I got pretty good at "down-the-river" and "box-baseball," but there were limits to what games you could play on the sidewalk. I didn't have a bike larger than a tricycle and wasn't allowed to ride a two-wheeler. We could not afford a day camp although one summer I snuck into a program at my public school until they threw me out for non-payment. What I did to occupy myself was read. It was my only pleasure and my only escape from isolation and loneliness.

Before the start of third grade I read 23 Hardy Boy books and several others besides. My new teacher asked everyone in the class, in turn, if any of us had read a single book over summer. When it was my turn to respond I recounted all of the books I had read. I received teasing from my classmates and a quizzical look of disbelief from a teacher who thought she had heard it all.

One book that struck a chord in me involved a young sailor in the great age of seafaring vessels. He got into one adventure after another, using his wiles to survive. In the end, he had to face a moral dilemma to save some strangers from certain death. His choice, the only one which made sense, resulted in the hero sacrificing himself and suffering a humiliating defeat in front of his peers. He lost a leg in the process and his seafaring dreams came to an end but the author led you to believe that he took the right action and had grown from this experience by accomplishing a greater good. The book unsettled me. I wondered what was to become of the protagonist next, as if he was going to pick up his life in some unwritten pages of another book. His life, as he dreamed it, was over. I didn't get a sense of where he would go, what he would do or how he would manage to live life on land, one which he was so unprepared for. I began to think that life was more like this book than I had previously imagined. I longed to read the unwritten pages of my life story. I wanted to think that there was hope for me like I believed there was for the brave sailor. I had clung to an unspoken but very real desire that my father would just disappear, and with him, my everyday sense of impending terror. I began to form an understanding that my life was just the way it was. And the probability of rescue, however intensely wished for, was unlikely. Slowly, the subject of my reading turned from fiction to philosophy and history. Was life nothing but the misery and the sense of isolation that I was feeling? How did people from ancient times cope with meaning in their lives? I began reading the large overview of philosophy series by Will and Muriel Durant. I couldn't keep track of the many ideas and began keeping index cards of quotations and thoughts from the great scholars. I expanded my readings into psychology when my brother became a psych major. I read many of his textbooks focusing my attention on theories of personality. Freud was a major attraction and I enjoyed reading his own words after reading so much that had been written about him. But this was just a stepping stone. When I found Jung I felt that for the first time I had found someone who had an inkling of the truth. I resonated with Jung. His notions of the collective unconscious, of anima and animus, were not just ideas to me. I felt them to be true. I especially enjoyed *Psyche and Symbol*.

    Autobiographies, notably Lawrence's *Seven Pillars of Wisdom* and Merton's *Seven Storey Mountain* (and later *The Autobiography of Malcolm X*), inspired me with the possibility that a person could not only take stock of one's life but take control of it. The little book, *six nonlectures* by e.e. cummings, became a hallmark of individuality and a mirror to me of everything I was not. Even *The Agony and the Ecstasy* by Irving Stone portrayed Michelangelo

Chapter 2. Into The World

as a person driven by his passion. I knew I had to find my passion in life and that once I did, it would pull me forward and give me direction and meaning.

Around the time of my high school years I discovered the existentialists. I was enamored with Camus. I completely identified with *The Stranger* and with K., the protagonist in *The Trial*. How could he know me so well? I saw my life as following the rules, paths and expectations set by others. I did not know who I was or what I wanted. This would have entailed knowing possibilities and having choice and I neither knew my possibilities nor felt I had meaningful choices. I was very aware of the only choice Camus thought possible for him. I read Kafka's Metamorphosis and was astounded not only by the power of his symbolism (I had never read anything like that before) but was frightened by my understanding of the story. I began to think that suicide might be the only creative and courageous act left for me.

Florida

One notable exception to the summer doldrums of my youth occurred in 1957 when I was eight years old. My father surprised us by taking us to the Dunes Motel on Collins Avenue in Miami for 2 weeks in August. In my mind, the larger than life Charioteer at the motel entrance will stand forever, although the Dunes is now long gone. We packed up the push-button Desoto as if we were never returning and took off down route 95 in the wee hours of the morning. Before this journey, I thought the New Jersey turnpike had been the most exotic place in the universe. What I loved most about this trip was stopping for lunch in the small towns on the way down and back and seeing the many different ways people lived their lives away from the squalor of the Bronx.

In a South Carolina town we shopped for toiletries in a Woolworth Department Store. I wandered away from my parents looking at the different products on the counters, marveling at the fountain service that long since disappeared in my neighborhood. I took a sip from a nearby water fountain and a black man hurriedly came over to me. "You can't do this," he said sternly, and held my gaze. I knew I was in scary territory. I quickly went into "father-mode:

> Say nothing.
> Listen to his words.
> Retrace your actions.
> Evaluate the context.
> Use your head...I drew a blank.

He pointed to a sign, high over my head that read, "Colored-Only."

"I didn't see it," I stammered.

He looked around, saw that no one else was paying attention to us and said, "I can tell you're not from around here. Be more careful next time." I scampered away, glad that some anonymous stranger was looking out for me.

That summer was also remarkable for chiggers, one of the wonders of creation. These vermin blessed my legs and my brother's neck and we came home with festering sores. It was only after Allen developed large infected sores and he went for treatment that I mentioned my problem. But by the time I said something, the infection had spread from my knee down to my ankle and I had a fever that wasn't going down. Dr. Friedenreich was called to examine me. He took one look at my green and purple leg and he gave my mother a look of astonishment. "Sadie (he was only one who ever called her by her real name) why didn't you call me sooner?" But he didn't expect an answer. He knew my mother wouldn't call unless it was an emergency. Who had money for doctor bills?

He disappeared into the kitchen with my mother and returned several minutes later. He told me that I should really be in the hospital but that he did not want to risk moving me. He also said that if he had been called any later, I would have been in danger of losing my leg. But he was going to take care of me. While he said this, he held his right hand behind his back, obviously holding something. My eyes never left his hand, my fear incredible. What was going to happen? My mother came forward with a rolled up towel and the doctor told me to bite down on it and to yell as much as I wanted. I took the towel between the teeth and my mother positioned herself on the bed holding down my leg with a grip so strong I didn't think it possible. Then the hand came forward and I saw the scalpel. I turned away in terror as he cut into my flesh and with his massive hands, forced out the pus through the large incisions.

When it was over I looked at the sheets covered with blood and vile smelling fluids and couldn't imagine that my leg was intact. Thankfully, the bandaging took longer than the carving as I needed the time to recover from the shock. The doctor ordered that I drink plenty of fluids, and for some reason, my mother gave me 7-Up almost exclusively. It must have been on sale. I drank so much that I couldn't stand to look at it for several years. I missed three weeks of school. Out of boredom, I not only kept up with my homework but I completely finished reading my schoolbooks, cover to cover, much to the amazement of my teacher. I recovered nicely and returned to school with no permanent damage to my leg.

Angels

I don't remember when my awareness of the angels left me. As a small child of four I felt the presence of two angels, one over each shoulder. I didn't see them, but in my quiet moments I thought of them as embodying the image of the Statue of Liberty, with rays of golden light emanating from behind their heads. I felt their protection and guidance, especially in times of stress or trouble. At these times I could wordlessly connect to them and feel a sense of calm.

Most of the time I wouldn't think about them, but when faced with difficulty, I would rely upon their sheltering warmth. A visualization would appear in my consciousness, a shimmering silver sea beneath a raging storm. A lick of golden wave would reach out and touch me, and I would feel a certainty that the difficulty would pass and everything would be alright. One day while I was alone in the house, I tried to balance one of my brother's stickball bats on the tips of my fingers. The presence of the angels popped up in my mind. Previously, their unbidden presence would mark a silent, unthinking command to stop whatever I was doing. That day, consciousness dawned and with it, a response of rebellion. I wasn't going to stop. I continued balancing the stick for several minutes, enjoying the sense of danger and bravado. And then I narrowly escaped disaster. I grew too confident in my newly found skill, walking around our apartment when the bat came flying out of my hand, hurtling towards the large fish tank in the hallway. I caught it by the tip but I could not stop my forward momentum. I ran into the stick as I planted it firmly against the wall. It scraped painfully against my thigh and left a large purple wound that stayed with me for weeks. I got the message.

Freddy

My parents were friendly with the other Jewish families in the building and were best friends with the Gold's on our floor. Harold Gold, who could have been Jimmy Durante's brother, worked in a toy store and would steal model cars and toys for his son Freddy every week. If this wasn't enough to make him a God in my eyes, I had only to look at how he adored his son. Harold and Mollie were older than my parents. But their children, Anita and Freddy were the same ages as Allen and me and this is probably

Chapter 2. Into The World

what forged the bond between the parents. For most of my youth, Freddy was my only friend.

It wasn't that Freddy did not like me or that we did not have some good times, but I was Freddy's friend only when he didn't have something better to do. He was small, fast, and athletic. I was pudgy, slow and not allowed in the street. He had a world of stickball and punchball and other kids. I played sidewalk games. Outside of the house, or especially when he was with other kids, he teased me mercilessly. When he would have anything to do with me at all, he would hit me and run away, daring me to catch him. On those few occasions when I did catch up to him I beat him up pretty good.

When Freddy turned 40 I was invited to attend his birthday party. We had not spoken to each other in years, but at his party I was amazed to discover the reverence with which he held me and astonished to hear such a different accounting of our childhood together. He remembered close times and had fond memories. He could have been talking about someone else. I simply smiled my way through these stories wondering how my memories of the past could have been so very different from his. It was another lesson about the power of perception and how it can shape a person's reality.

Mr. Jefferson

Mr. Jefferson was the super of our building. He collected our garbage from the dumbwaiter which still worked when I was young, shoved coal into the furnace and shoveled snow from the building's entrance in the winter and did what he could to keep the 1880's building in good repair. My parents never said an unkind word about Mr. Jefferson and they always gave him a present at Christmas. He was considerably older than they were, was medium height, stocky and had gray about his temples. He had an even disposition, enjoyed the children of the building and never had an unkind word for them. I never knew if there was a Mrs. Jefferson, but from time to time he was visited by his son, Roy. Roy was a classy guy with uncommon good looks. You could just tell he loved his father and had respect for him which is the way I felt too.

Mr. Jefferson lived in a windowless apartment in the subbasement of the building. There was no direct way to get there. Around the right side of the building was a long ramp leading down to a large enclosed area that was the resting place for the building's garbage cans. Mr. Jefferson would roll the rusty cans up the ramp on collection day and roll the empties back down. A little to the right of this area was a cut out through the building that led to the fenced, partially weeded, but mostly broken up pavement that was the stage for the building's backside. It was a totally enclosed area bounded by surrounding buildings. It was impossible not to peer into the unseen lives of what seemed like countless apartments. There was always movement by the windows, shadows on drawn shades, and occasionally someone watching you. It always frightened me to be there. It was here that there was a doorless opening to our building with two paths. One led to a small area that had a washing machine and seemed to be the Mecca of every bug in the Bronx. I don't know if we ever used these machines. In fact, I have no memories of washes ever being made! The other path led to the door to Mr. Jefferson's apartment. I was only inside once, but I was amazed how large it was and how well it was furnished. With one look around I realized that there was a lot more to Mr. Jefferson than any of us understood.

Mr. Jefferson was a Negro. I don't know what made me see that difference for the first time. In a flash, a curtain of innocence fell from my eyes, and the unspoken understanding which had been like a cloudy haze, came into focus. All the hateful things I heard my father say, all the stories about segregation in the South, all the crime in the news, all the conditioned fear that was poised to take hold,

Chapter 2. Into The World

all became known in one terrifying moment. I had always harbored suspicion, even contempt for these Negroes that I had yet to come across. And now I knew that something inside was changed. I was filled with sorrow for the Negroes and for myself. My sense of injustice was born and I feared that I would forever see only differences in people. I felt that something truly horrible had happened to me with this newfound knowledge and I cried.

What restored my equilibrium was my love for Willie Mays. Willie, who was my hero, was so much more than the color of his skin. All the things I admired about him, his love for baseball, his zeal for excellence, his ability to come through at clutch moments, were contrary to the ingrained notions of stereotype and programmed hatred I did not yet know I possessed. As I never felt anything but idol worship for Willie, I knew there was hope that I could overcome the prejudices ingrained since childhood.

5th grade

I had a loud booming voice when I was young. When a group of kids were talking, I would be the one likely to get singled out and into trouble. By the time I was in 5th grade, I was used to this. But I had not run into the likes of Mrs. Debutari. She fingered me from the start as one of the bad boys, and try as I might, I couldn't shake her. I was one of the nice, sweet, respectful children who followed instructions and didn't give the teachers lip. I figured she knew this, but she relied on my meekly accepting her discipline while she couldn't get away disciplining the really bad boys who would defy her authority and make her look bad. To make matters worse, she sent home a note to my parents stating that I had failed to hand in some homework assignments. I would be thinking about my funeral arrangements had I not been so angry. This was simply not true. My mom came to school for one of those famous parent-teacher conferences. Mrs. D. was as sweet and phony as she could be, but she quickly solved the problem. She asked me what the assignment was for the following day and I defiantly said that she didn't give one. She pointed to a corner of the blackboard and asked me to read it. "Read what?" I asked. The following Saturday, mom brought me to a store that looked like a repository for used shoeboxes. This store belonged to Mr. Feigenbaum, the optometrist. He didn't look like any doctor I had ever seen and I couldn't imagine him cutting people up and doing the bloody things that doctors do. I had also heard that eye doctors put things in your eyes and I was scared. But during my examination he just fiddled with all his dials and lenses. He told us that I was severely near-sighted.

When I put on my first pair of glasses I was filled with rage and disbelief. Not because I could see clearly for the first time, that was pretty spectacular, but because I realized all that I had missed in life. Suddenly I understood why I was such a lousy ball player, why I needed to sit up front at the movies and make a score of other adjustments that I hadn't been aware I was making. And I cried because of all the people around me throughout my childhood, no one picked up on this but horrible old Mrs. D.

But this miracle of gaining normal eyesight was soon to be topped by another. Mrs. Debutari retired. My whole class rejoiced and the naughty ones took pride that they were instrumental in putting her over the edge. They had found their purpose and felt their new power. A new teacher, Ms. Cohen took over the class and I returned to good graces. She was everything Mrs. D. was not. She was right out of school, young, pretty, idealistic and completely unaware of what was facing her. The class bullies found their new sport and were determined to do her in. Ms. Cohen did not return the next year. Through some quirks of administrative oversight, this same core group of kids, including me, managed to stay together through the 6th, 7th and 8th grades. At the end of the 6th grade, Mrs.

Chapter 2. Into The World

Chafetz called it quits, at the end of the 7th, Mrs. Grossman retired, stating that she had never seen a group like us before. At the end of the 8th grade, Ms. Farrell, another new recruit, left teaching entirely. Five for five.

Having my new glasses and restored to good-boy status, I thought that my life as a juvenile delinquent was behind me. That is, until I was brought down to Mr. Kligman's office. I waited for him outside the hall. He came out and looked very sternly at me. He told me that someone had seen me set a fire to the garbage can of used milk containers and I was in serious trouble. I was to wait in his office until he returned. Inside, a Spanish kid was already waiting. I had seen him around school, but didn't know him. We both sat in silence for what seemed a long time. If it hadn't been so quiet, I would not have heard the small sound that came from Mr. Kligman's desk. And then something clicked in my brain and I understood what was happening.

If I was called into the office about the fire, then this kid must have been also. He was my accuser. And the small sound I heard was from Mr. Kligman's intercom. There must have been a small crowd in another room, listening. I wasn't going to disappoint.

"You here about the fire?" I began innocently.

"Oh yeah," he said confidently. "You did it. I saw you!"

"Now how can that be," I said sarcastically for my audience, "You know I didn't do it. You must have done it yourself!"

And he replied, "So what? You gonna prove it?"

Bingo. I was whisked away and told to return to my class. The Spanish kid never returned and was rumored to have been sent to the feared "500 school" for the really bad students. I never was really worried. I didn't know how to light a match.

Jesus

I knew very little about Jesus. I knew we did not celebrate Christmas and I knew that when not in public, my father would say that Jesus was a phony and the perpetrator of the biggest fraud on mankind. And those were the kind words. I felt very uncomfortable with the notion of Jesus as the Son of God. But I felt an attraction towards Jesus that was as unmistakable as it was frightening to a young Jewish boy. As I got older, I went to a few church services to see what it was like, but I was turned off by the Church and its liturgy. I applied my method of choice for discovering most things about the world: I read. I read the New Testament, Chardin, Merton, and a bunch of pop books on the market. One book had an engaging title, "Are You Running With Me, Jesus?" It portrayed the power of faith and belief without the trappings of religion. It appealed to me in a way Jewish Orthodox tradition and church services did not. Still, I could not embrace Jesus as my savior and did not yet feel a complete connection with my spirituality.

Roaches

Something magical happened when I turned 10. I was suddenly allowed to stay by myself without a supervising presence. On Fridays my father met up with the only guy that could put up with him, my mother played cards with the neighbors and my brother did what boys do with their friends. I was home alone. Tired of Broderick Crawford on *Highway Patrol* and repeats of *Twilight Zone*, and having no computer games to practice my commando skills, I created my own virtual reality. I filled the bathroom sink with water and gathered my supplies: a paper plate, a paper cup, and last, a luger water gun that held a lot of water for its day. I sat down in the bathroom, waiting for my prey. It did not take long for those big old roaches to start

Chapter 2. Into The World

roaming the walls. I'd pick a big one and capture it under the cup. Then I'd slip the paper plate under it and take it to the sink, where I would dump it in the water. Roaches are not great swimmers so I had time to position myself. Slowly they would reach the edge, where the water met the sink, and try to gain a foothold onto dry land. Sometimes I would let them crawl up a bit, and then I would zap them back into the water with my water gun. If it was a fast bugger, then one roach could last me for hours. If they were not adept, I would need a few to keep me busy. When I was tired and ready for sleep I would drain the water and watch them try to get away. They were so feeble that they had little fight left and washed away down the drain. Not one ever escaped.

6th grade

I was a bit of an enigma to my teachers: I would do well on one test that all the kids did poorly on and then bomb an easy one; I was bored and would not pay attention in class but generally produced good quality work when I put my mind to it; I hardly ever spoke up in class but often knew the answer when called upon; my reading scores were quite high but I would perform below expectation on other standardized tests. I remember the day when an administrator came to discuss which kids would go into the 2 year SP (Special Progress) class enabling you to skip the 8th grade and which kids would go into the newly formed 3-year SP which didn't skip a grade. It was clear they were talking about me but the Administrator wanted to get a good look at me. I was asked to stand and then turn to my right.

Horror upon horrors: as many left handed people, I had to learn to cope in a right handed world. I wrote with my left but threw a ball and batted righty and did most other things right-handed. To this day, I have trouble distinguishing my right from my left although I cover for it better now. Instinctively, I know my left hand and then make the connection to my right when needed. I wasn't as quick as a kid. I began turning left and with this turn, left behind my chances for the SP, at least for two years.

Stoppage of time

My first clue that the universe wasn't playing with a full deck happened when I was 10 years old and at the movies. No, it wasn't a sci-fi thriller, though I loved *The Incredible Shrinking Man*. I went to the concession stand and ran back to my seat through the dark aisles and fell, face forward. As I fell, clutching my popcorn and my drink, time slowed. My feet were off the ground and I floated in a peaceful space for what seemed a very long time. The events of my young life flashed by me as if I was watching a slide show. Then I hit the ground and got a bloody nose. In an attempt to clear my breathing, I inadvertently pushed the blood all over my face. The movie people were more upset than I was and thought I had broken my nose. They took me to the office and I was afraid they were going to call my parents. I ran away when the bleeding stopped. I felt I had learned something important from this experience, though I didn't know what. Years later I discussed this phenomenon with a psychiatrist friend of mine. He suggested that fear, or some related factor, speeds up the processing faculties of the mind. The perception of the mind working so fast, he continued, gives the impression of time slowing down. While this may be a plausible explanation, while I was falling, I wasn't looking for one. I had experienced another way of understanding myself in a world where time was relative. It felt natural, not funny or wrong. I was sure that others had felt the same way as I did but did not talk about it to anyone.

— 3 —
Crossing Tremont

Dream

I am walking on the street near my old elementary school. Perhaps I am walking home after school. It is the end of day and the sun is going down fast. A group of boys appear out from the shadows of a building and encircle me. The leader of the group, a big strong kid steps into the circle with me and starts to taunt me. At first I don't respond but this only makes him angry. I am making him look bad before his buddies. I decide to speak with him, to see if I can deflect his barrage of insults. This gets nowhere and he takes a long roundhouse swipe at the back of my head. I am jolted sideways to the sound of laughter all around me.

Suddenly, I am conscious. I am awake in my dream and I realize that I have had this same dream where this same boy beats me up every night for weeks. In the flash of an instant I realize that it does not have to end the same way. I lunge with a punch and hit him squarely on the jaw. He staggers back, more from surprise than hurt, and I hit him again and again.

Chapter 3. Crossing Tremont

44

JHS 44 was seven long blocks from my house across Tremont Avenue, the wide two lane thoroughfare bustling with traffic. My solo crossing of Tremont catapulted me out of a constricted four block childhood into a new phase of physical and psychological independence. The world opened up to me and I was free to explore it. It was always important to look like you knew where you were going. There was always someone around who would pick a fight for what you were carrying in your pockets. If you looked frightened or lost, you were dead meat.

One day I wandered into a Spanish enclave. It was clear I didn't belong and I was getting too much attention from some of the bigger kids in the street. I wanted to run, fearing that I would be beaten up just for sport but I knew that I would never make it to the end of the block. Running would have tipped them off that I was scared. So I held myself erect, walked with a brisk pace and tried to appear confident but I didn't make it. A guy stopped me and some of his friends were drawing closer. You bet I was scared. But then Juan showed up. He was the new kid in class. He didn't speak much English and he looked like he needed a friend, so I looked out for him. On his turf Juan was clearly in control and he introduced me as his friend. His word was good enough for the other kids and they backed off. I stayed around for a while before high tailing back to familiar ground, gaining new respect for Juan having met him in his element.

Caste System

Grade schools and junior high worked on the caste system. Classes were assigned numbers from "1" to whatever. The smartest kids were in the "1" class. Freddy was there. I was in the "2" class. The lower the number, the whiter and more Jewish, the higher the number…well, you just kept away from those kids. Freddy would lord his supremacy over me at every opportunity. "You're the best of the rest," was a constant refrain. Freddy did not make the traditional SP class but was selected for the new three-year, SP3 class in 7th grade. With two specialized classes in front of me, I was now assigned to the "7-1" class. A distinction of no honor.

Music

At the end of the 6th grade all the students were ushered into the auditorium. We were all handed a test paper with blank boxes and told to listen carefully. "Which note was higher, which lower?" I didn't understand what the purpose of this test was. I did what I was told because that's the kind of kid I was. I listened, answered the questions and thought nothing of it. Until I entered the 7th grade and I was put in music class on my first day. The teacher asked what instrument I wanted to play. I would attend music class almost every day and would not attend the fun classes like electrical or woodworking shop like most of the other boys. What I was later to find out was that I was the only kid in the whole district that answered all the questions correctly. I had to make a choice and I didn't even know the sound of many of the instruments. And there was no turning back once instruments were distributed. I would be stuck with my choice for better or worse. I looked around to see what some of the other boys picked and selected the trumpet. I could tell by some of the envious groans from the boys who hadn't selected yet that I made the right choice.

I received an old, dented case with the trumpet obviously jiggling inside, forms that I had to bring home for my parents to sign noting that they were accountable for the trumpet if it got lost or damaged, a new mouthpiece, another form asking for money for the mouthpiece, and

Chapter 3. Crossing Tremont

an instruction book that I had to guard with my life because it could not be replaced. The worst part was that I was told I had to bring the trumpet home every night to practice and bring it back to school daily for class. I was not thrilled and wished that I had done poorly on that test back in 6th grade.

I opened the case and was assaulted by a burst of smells that were fermenting over the summer. The old, dented silverish horn lay in a garden of mold that grew on the inner walls of the case. I took the trumpet apart, pulling out all the valves and unscrewing any part that was capable of coming loose. Congealed valve fluid and a ubiquitous green slime covered the valves and slides. I threw everything back in the case and took the assemblage home. I filled up the sink with water and whatever cleaners were underneath my mother's sink and soaked the trumpet for hours while I did major surgery on the trumpet case. Thus began my surprising love affair with music.

Once I saw how demanding the string instruments were, I was immensely happy with my choice. It seemed that half the class was devoted to tuning what would not be tuned on a string instrument. Put a finger or two down on a trumpet valve, blow and you got your note. Not so the hapless violins. I made good progress and soon my friend Joe and I were both designated first trumpets with Joe sitting in the first chair. This was fine with me. I loved playing as part of the orchestra, but I was petrified if only the brass were playing or, God forbid, I had to play alone. Then Joe and some other kids started showing up with their own new instruments and when I didn't take the hint, my teacher started laying on the guilt. Either I was serious about the trumpet and would convince my parents to purchase a new instrument for me or, perhaps I didn't want to be in the orchestra? I hounded my mother whenever my father wasn't around and was astounded when my father came home one day with a brass beauty that he paid $45 for. I was in heaven. I continued playing trumpet for the remaining two years in junior high.

As 9th graders and seniors we accompanied the drama club's production of the musical Oklahoma! We practiced all year for this, and on opening night my mother and brother came. I felt electricity in the air. I had never looked forward to anything like this before and never felt the anxious thrill of performance. But there was one section I dreaded where Joe and I had to play a section of high notes together for the song, "Surrey on Top." I knew it would be hit or miss. Suddenly, the orchestra was playing and I felt that for the first time we were really making music. Everything was going beautifully. Then reality dawned as the hard part approached. I was playing the tune with all eyes on me. Mr. Salter was raising his hand ever so gently telling me to play louder. But Joe was nowhere to be heard. He stared straight ahead at his music, his fingers went through the motions but his horn made no sound. At the end of the piece I was triumphant and I could not wait to speak to my mother and Allen to see if they heard me. They did and I was so proud of myself.

Joe, however, was crushed. At our next class, he told me to take the first trumpet seat, that he didn't deserve it anymore. I had never seen such a happy-go-lucky kid so serious. There was no arguing with him, I had come through in the heat of performance and he didn't. I switched seats but we both knew he was the better player. One of the teachers encouraged me to get private lessons. I broached this with my mother, and lobbied hard, but my father would not hear of it. "You learn in school, don't you?" And without waiting for a response, he gave his own reply, "that's enough." End of discussion.

Soon after our performance, a few of the kids, with the assistance of a teacher, started a dance band. We practiced before and after school and during lunch. I insisted that Joe take the first chair. On the day of our performance before the school in the auditorium our teacher

Chapter 3. Crossing Tremont

brought out new music stands that had been donated by a bandleader friend of his. The stands were so low that I could hardly see the music. I muddled through on memory alone and it was not my best effort. As a group, though, we had a successful show. After this performance the members of our band gained a certain following as kids gathered outside the door of the music room to hear us play. I felt like a rock star, but no one, especially any of the girls, gave me any extra attention.

Graduation approached and I was filled with anxiety. The ceremony was to begin with the trumpet's call to arms. Who was going to do it, Joe or me? I practiced day and night for weeks but I knew I could not do it without mistakes and was petrified lest I get the nod. One Sunday afternoon close to graduation I turned on the Yankee game on TV. I heard someone in the crowd of fans playing the call to arms. I knew it was Joe and I listened intently. He was flawless. Right before the graduation ceremony was to begin, Mr. Salter picked Gerald to play the solo. I was so relieved. He did a fine job and received good recognition for his efforts. As part of the musical program, the orchestra played "Softly, as in a Morning Sunrise." It was magnificent. I didn't know it then, but my trumpet career came to an end that day as I did not continue my musical studies in high school or college.

Term Paper

Music wasn't the only surprise awaiting me at junior high school. There were so many challenges to overcome. There were teachers with subject matter expertise. I knew I had to prove myself academically and socially all over again. There were raised academic expectations and my very first term paper was due at the end of the year. I picked the topic of ancient Greece. It was so far away and seemed so sophisticated and important compared to life on 178th street.

Learning how to do research and to write a term paper were skills that we would need throughout high school and college, the teachers explained, and we had better learn how to do it. Papers would routinely be required in the 8th and 9th grades, let alone high school and college. My whole academic record appeared to hinge on how well I completed this assignment. Fear, never far from my consciousness, motivated me to walk the 8 long blocks across Southern Boulevard to the Westchester Farms branch library each Saturday after Children's Services at the shul. It soon became my haven. A place to escape from home, a place to relax, surrounded by all those glorious books. Fear gave way to fascination and I became enthralled with my subject and perhaps more importantly, eager to learn my way around the library. By the end of the term I received an "A" for my paper with a small note in the margin saying, "Great job with this." From that moment I never received less than an "A" in any research paper I wrote in junior high, high school, college or grad school. With each good grade, my confidence soared. Research and paper writing became skills that would serve me all my life.

Education

The students I met in seventh and eighth grade classes were an education unto themselves. I met smart kids who weren't Jewish, boys who worked besides their fathers in stores before and after school, girls who were blatantly sexy, boys who carried knives and used them, kids that wore torn clothing and shoes with holes in them, kids that hardly spoke English and kids that were considerably more well off than we were. There were many new experiences of discovery, some rather painful. I'll never forget the day Elvia came to school after being raped by the father of her friend, or when Louis was sent to a special school after he stabbed his uncle for abusing him, or when Errol died when he was hit in the street by a drunk

Chapter 3. Crossing Tremont

driver, or the look of shame on Regina's face when Barry told the boys that he had sex with her.

I became the homeroom rep to the student government, G.O. No one in my class volunteered and I was appointed because our home room teacher probably guessed that I wouldn't put up a fuss. Once a month the selected reps would have to give up our lunch hour and eat our sandwich in silence while being told some new rule the school was enforcing. In the eighth grade, Mr. Brown, the program counselor, had the school "adopt" a poor kid from one of the international save the kid programs. The reps were responsible for squeezing money out of their classmates. I got up each week and asked. I was not a great salesman, but the force of repetition eventually wore down the stingiest kids. Before long, our class was the leading contributor. One day Mr. Brown received one of the standard thank you letters from the sponsoring agency. He gave it to me to read to the class. As I was greeted with whoops and cheers, I realized that the letter was addressed directly to Mr. Brown and that there was no mention of the school program or the many student contributors. I ran into him in the hallway and asked him about this. He brusquely waved me aside and told me that he would speak to me about this some other time. But that time never came. I stopped asking the kids for money and soon the program lost momentum and folded.

8th grade and Paper Route

When I entered the 8th grade it was time for me to work. My father had worked all his life. My brother worked a variety of after-school jobs and now it was my turn to learn responsibility and get acquainted with the real world, or so my father said. My father made it clear that he would cover basic expenses like food and clothing, but if I wanted something extra, like a soda, I would have to earn my own personal spending money. I was to get a paper route.

That's how my brother started and there was no discussion about alternatives.

Only in the last year was I allowed to cross the great divide of Tremont Avenue alone, and that was to get to school. Now, I had to disrupt my routine of cookies, milk and television, put off doing my homework until the evening, go to a new neighborhood, deal with strangers, and face the laughter and scorn of Freddy and others who teased me for being forced to work while they played after school. Worst of all, I felt so afraid and didn't know why. I appealed to my mother who argued vigorously with my father. But she lost, as she lost most other petitions. I was convinced that I would hate this job.

My brother brought me down to the small storefront that served as the distribution point for the local deliveries of the NY Post. I was assigned a route and was shown where all the buildings were. From that point on I would be on my own. The manager urged me to purchase a paper carrier that most of the kids used. I went back to my father and asked him for the money, but to save a couple of bucks, he constructed a hideous looking basket made from the remains of my mother's defunct folding supermarket wagon and a canvas bag. It was functional, though it had very sharp edges and looked ridiculous. Those delivery boys that cared at all to notice laughed at me every time they saw it.

There was always some promotion going on to cajole us to get new customers. Each new subscription would give us points that we could redeem for prizes. A big poster was put up to graph our success and stimulate competition. Some kids really went all out. But I didn't care. Not only did I not want to be there, I wasn't going to spend five minutes more than necessary on anything related to the paper business. The store manager was quick to pick up on my attitude and frequently gave me a list of addresses to canvass and would ask me how I did the day before. "No luck," I would say, and flash him a grin, "No

Chapter 3. Crossing Tremont

one wants this lousy paper." One day he was ready for me. We began the routine as usual but then he marched me to his desk. He took out his keys from his pocket, unlocked his desk drawer and removed the phone. He had a bunch of telephone numbers and he said matter-of-factly, "We'll see if you did this canvassing or not." He called the first number. No response. He called the second. No response and I began to breathe easier. He called the third and began talking. "No one came to your door," he repeated to the voice on the other end of the phone, "are you sure of that?" A broad smile came across his face. And then I thought how I had been saved by the first two phone calls. "Wait a minute," I interrupted, "ask him if he was indoors the entire day or if he left the house for any reason." I waited until this question was relayed and died the proverbial thousand deaths until the answer came back. " Well, he did go down to get the mail about 4:30," said the manager. "That's when I was there," I said. "And don't ever question me like this again!"

To save time along the route, which was spread out over of 12 blocks, I picked up a hint from my brother and traveled across rooftops. This way I didn't have to climb up to the top floor of each building. I would take enough papers for two buildings, climb up one, cross the roof, and come down the other.

A small group of hoods began to follow me and terrorize me along the route, threatening to steal my papers and rob me. I kept away as much as I could, but eventually, they caught up to me. At worst, they stole a few papers, but I escaped with my skin intact. At one encounter, I drew my wagon behind me in a protective stance. A sharp projection of steel from underneath the make-shift wagon went deep into my skin at the back of my heel. I began to hobble and bleed. Once the toughs saw what was happening they howled with laughter, called me whatever clever names they could think of at the moment, but left me alone to curse my wounds.

The cut was deep and soon became infected. I hid it from my parents for as long as I could, but by the time my mother noticed, I could hardly walk. Reluctantly, my father agreed that I could not deliver papers like this. He accused me of self inflicting the wound to get out of work. He called me a shirker, irresponsible, lazy, a good-for-nothing and told me I would never amount to anything. I had trouble following him in his fury and began to zone out but I knew I had to stand my ground and pay attention lest I miss a question. I was clearly contemptible in his eyes. He felt nothing but scorn for me. Once again I had proved his worst fears for me. I didn't measure up. I was nothing.

Bar Mitzvah

Hebrew school was not on my father's radar. He wanted me to attend, do well, not get into trouble and get Bar Mitzvahed like all his brother's and sister's kids. He also had no idea what I was learning and couldn't care less. When it came time to receive Bar Mitzvah instruction I chose my old first and second grade teacher, Mrs. Bitter, to guide me through the prayers. This went somewhat against custom as most of the teachers of the older grades usually got the honor and the extra bucks. The Hebrew came easily to me and I learned all my prayers and melodies in three weeks. By the time of my Bar Mitzvah, almost eight months away, I had it all memorized. The melodies rang through me. But singing in the shower was one thing and singing before the whole congregation was another. When I was called up to the pulpit, a place I had never been, I realized something I should have known before. I was going to stand facing the arc with my back to the congregation. This calmed me down and I proceeded on auto pilot. On either side of me were old, holy men, practiced in swaying to and fro, who often prayed in whispers and at breakneck speed. From time to time they looked at me as I went through my motions. I knew I had impressed them. Every word

Chapter 3. Crossing Tremont

was pronounced correctly and sung in the proper melody with perfect inflection and nuance. I recognized admiration in their eyes. I was about three quarters through my haftorah when I purposely made a mistake I knew only they would recognize. I sang a word in the wrong melody and I looked at them to let them know that I knew it. I finished up and, as was custom, received the pelting of bags of candy from the sharpshooters in the first row. I then awaited Rabbi Charlops' speech to "my dear Bar Mitzvah boy" which I had heard hundreds of times before. He had several stock themes and I wondered which one he would pull out on this occasion. Only this time it was different.

It was clear to me that Rabbi Charlop had done some homework on me. He knew my history as a student and praised me in the most glowing terms before the whole congregation. I was stunned but grateful. But as he was winding up, Rabbi Charlop said something I never heard him say before. He implored me to continue my Jewish education and go to Hebrew High School. He paused and I understood what it meant to have life literally drain out from you. I was overwhelmed with the possibility of going to Hebrew High School. If I had the energy to muster a response I would have said yes, not because I wanted to, but because I did not have the strength to go against such a powerful authority figure. But I didn't respond and he went on to conclude his remarks.

After the ceremony we had a catered affair and I received lots of envelopes with checks. For a brief moment I relished the idea that all this cash was going to be mine. When it was all over, we gathered all the gifts together in the living room. My mother wrote down a description of each gift or amount next to a printed guest list while my father was in charge of insulting the cheapness of each giver with every invective at his command. When it was all over, he simply took all the money away, saying, "You didn't think this was yours, did you? How did you think we were going to pay for this affair?"

Science Bound

At the end of the eighth grade several boys took the admittance test and were accepted to Brooklyn Tech, one of the specialized high schools in the city. This, combined with the growing exodus of the middle class out of the Bronx, left some glaring vacancies in the 9SP3 class in my school. They needed some kids to fill the empty seats and I was asked if I wanted to go. A back door into respectability was unexpectedly opened and I grabbed it. Freddy's words, written into my school yearbook, remain for posterity: "You can't be a doofus because you are coming into my class."

Up until then, schoolwork and grades were things only my father was interested in. I had maintained an 85 average just by showing up. Now for the first time, I felt challenged to show the other kids that I could be just as good as them and to show the school that this was where I belonged in the first place. I did well in math, science and music, which for me was a major subject, and I was the favorite of my English teacher. I was the brother of Allen, the darling of her class 6 years earlier, and I inherited an anticipation of greatness that was only matched by her blind affection for me. My work was only mediocre. I never received a grade in English higher than 85 in the previous 2 years of junior high school or in the three years of high school that followed. But she loved me and, as it turned out, my brother did not disappoint.

The class had to write an autobiography as the major assignment for the year. It was time to hand it in and I was in a panic. We had months to write it and I didn't have a word. I could hardly bear the pain of self-reflection. My existence was defined by insecurity. I felt no sense of self, just fear. Fear of triggering the wrath of the capricious God that was my father. Life was a progression of expectations that always left me falling short. How could I write this? I turned in tears to my brother for help. He wrote a very engaging autobiography that earned outlandish praise and

Chapter 3. Crossing Tremont

a 95 from my adoring teacher. At the end of the year I was only one of a handful in my class that made Honor Roll with a 90 average. Freddy wasn't one of them. It was, however, a short-lived sweetness.

We all took the entrance exam to Bronx Science, one of the elite high schools in the city. My motivation was simple. Avoid going to Roosevelt High, the site of my brother's greatest academic achievements when the school enjoyed a better reputation. It had turned into an unruly hangout of tough guys awaiting jail or their draft papers in the six years since Allen had been there. Besides, everyone else in the smart classes took the test. It was the leveling plane. If Freddy got in and I didn't, my 9th grade average wouldn't be worth a damn. To my amazement, I was accepted. But so was Freddy and all the other smart kids in class. My pride and my fear knew no bounds. I would have the summer to mentally prepare myself for the greatest challenge of my life. At least I thought I'd be prepared, until I had a casual conversation with Ms. Smith, my science and homeroom teacher.

I came up to class one warm spring lunchtime as I usually did, to open the high windows with a long jump pole, clean the blackboard and the erasers, and straighten things up that needed straightening. This afternoon started no differently than any other. Ms. Smith made small talk with me, but on this day, I noted a slight change in the tone of her voice as she shifted to a new topic of conversation. She began recounting the number of kids that had made Science, but had left me out of the mix. When I reminded her that I also was going, in a voice dripping with disbelief, she asked slowly and deliberately, "And what are you going to do there, Michael?" That moment I tottered. And for the next three years, I never regained my balance. The ninth grade had been a year of firsts for me. I received recognition for playing the trumpet, I made Honor Roll and I proved to myself and to the other kids that I belonged in the SP class. But to

Ms. Smith, a teacher I liked and respected, I didn't stack up. I felt that my growing confidence was only a sham. She had seen through me. All my feelings of doubt and unworthiness bubbled to the surface once again.

To my father, admission to Science meant vindication. His advice that hard work would pay off bore fruit. At heart, I knew I had gotten lucky on the test and had to be at the bottom of the barrel of the 400 accepted boys. My brother wasn't always going to be there to bail me out. I recalled Ms. Smith's question and asked myself the one over and over again. What was I going to do there anyway?

Prom

Almost imperceptibly, the last days of ninth grade brought about a transformation to the class. Most of the kids had been together for years and the realization that something special was ending brought unspoken sadness and closeness. The prom was approaching and the girls, in their wisdom, knew that the boys would be helpless. The cabal got together and matched everyone with a partner. The girls came in two's and three's and surrounded each boy. They were very businesslike. This was not a date, they assured me. The whole class was going to the prom and I was going to the prom, period. This was not a choice and I was going with...(I held my breath)...Rebecca. I smiled at their selection. They matched me with a Jewish girl, just slightly taller than me. I had active fantasies about half the girls in class but the well-endowed Rebecca wasn't one of them. Still I liked her and it wasn't a date, anyway. I would have died to take Linda Watanabe. Linda, who was rumored to be sexually active with a gang member, Thurston, ending up going to the prom alone. When I asked why, she said that her conservative Japanese parents would kill her if she went out on a date and, besides, Thurston would not allow her to go with anyone other than him.

Chapter 3. Crossing Tremont

I have no memories of the prom itself, held in the gym, but I do remember that afterwards we all went on buses to Jahn's ice cream parlor on Fordham Road. I had never felt such a sense of belonging and acceptance. We stayed until some of the boys got thrown out for having a food fight which only added to the fun. I took Rebecca home, kissed her gently on the lips (she did not open her mouth) and wandered about the streets going in the general direction of school, not wanting the evening to end. To my surprise I saw Linda and approached her. I asked her if I could walk her home and she said yes. This was as close to a date that I would have for years. She lived about a half mile from school and I felt exhilarated and wilted by the time we arrived at her apartment building. I walked her up to her door and was about to kiss her good night when Thurston came out of nowhere brandishing a knife. He screamed at Linda and glared at me. When he regained some measure of self control he ordered Linda inside but she didn't budge. He told me to leave, pointing the knife in my direction and I did. I never felt that Linda was in any danger. The knife was for my benefit. But I was in no position to stand up to Thurston. I left quietly, feeling sad for Linda, and cried as I walked home. Linda and I never spoke about this in the few remaining weeks we had left in school.

The organizers of the prom arranged for a Saturday trip to Playland. Not everybody from our class went but we had a great time. Why didn't we get together like this all year round? After this, a smaller group met a few times in Crotona Park, just to hang out. My feeling of belonging lasted for a few weeks longer. Then graduation day came and we all went our separate ways.

Handball

When I was 15, my father got transferred for the summer to a small cheese plant in the Catskills. They paid for our bungalow and I was sworn to secrecy lest this financial arrangement be disclosed to anyone. All the kids went to the bungalow camp, except me. My father would not pay the extra cash as this would come out of his pocket. When someone asked me, in his presence, why I didn't go, dad replied that I didn't want to. I had to go along with this lie even though I longed for friends and activities. People could not understand that I would prefer to be alone and tried to convince me all summer to join up. At one point, my father even tried to convince me that it was what I wanted! Nevertheless, I was used to being alone and it sure beat the Bronx pavements, at least for one summer.

I became interested in handball that summer and played with anyone. We played with Spaldeens for that was the ball we had. On the weekdays, when the court was empty, I taught myself to hit the ball with my left hand. By the end of the summer, I was quite competent and developed a good sense of anticipation to complement my newly found quickness. A year later, when I first met my good friend Gary in our development in Queens, I found out that he also played. We teamed up as partners and never lost a doubles game in the next three years, until he went off to college. It was the only athletic achievement in my life.

Rochdale

The neighborhood had been changing for years. Changing meant that the white, Jewish families were moving away and non-white, mostly Puerto Ricans were moving in. My father was very much aware of this "element" and was quick to tell me that he wasn't prejudiced as he cursed the Negroes and anyone else who was different for the rising crime rate, dirty streets and other social ills. Still, he put up with the indignities as rent in our three bedroom apartment was cheap. Two events helped push him over

Chapter 3. Crossing Tremont

the edge. One was that my brother was graduating college and going off to grad school, so we didn't need a third bedroom. The other was that a new tenant moved into the building who had large German Shepherds. He let one of his dogs crap in the stairway. I was surprised that my father didn't kill him for it, but maybe it was the Shepards that stopped him.

We moved a few months into my first term at Science to a brand new development a few miles south of Kennedy airport. Like most decisions, my father did not need anyone's advice about where to move. He simply did what he thought best. It was a brand new building, had built-in air conditioning and was set in a park-like surrounding. When he announced we were leaving, I feared mostly for my mother. Her mother lived a few blocks away and they saw each other almost daily. Her sister was just a bus ride away from where we lived. Ma didn't drive and I feared the new isolation would make her drinking worse. I had no idea about what kind of commute I was going to have, but this too, was an annoyance I would have to deal with. The biggest, unanticipated change for me was my brother's moving away to grad school. My reliance upon him was so strong and our bond so close, that I could not imagine what life would be like without him giving me support and showing me the way. On the drive back from the airport to see him off I felt as if a part of me had been ripped out. I felt desolate. Several times in the coming months I called him from payphones, holding back the tears, to ask him for advice or just to hear his voice. We could never speak privately from home as phone calls to Texas were a major family event and were expensive. From time to time, he would send me funny letters which also helped lift my spirits a little, but didn't completely ease my loneliness.

I saw Rochdale as the first opportunity in life to recreate myself and meet new friends. But after several months I hardly met anyone new as I did not go to the local high school. I felt shut out and alone, not entirely new feelings for me. Two of the friends I did make were boys who went to other specialized high schools in the city. Gary went to Stuyvesant and Howie went to Brooklyn Tech. I also made friends with Rick but the four of us never clicked well together as a group. I stayed with my parents in Rochdale Village for six years.

Science

The trip to Bronx Science was two hours away on public transportation. With a bit of encouragement, I might have been persuaded to go to the local high school and save myself three years of misery, but after all the build up, I didn't have the moral fiber to truly consider the possibility. I entered Science as scared as a human being could be. Although several of my junior high friends also made Science, I never shared one class with them and hardly saw them. Not knowing a soul, feeling stupid and unprepared, I began my high school career without my biggest source of support, my brother.

My high school career was formed that fall in Math and French classes and was sealed the following year in English and Science Technique Lab, or STL, as it was called. My math teacher was an old, irritable, but caring soul. In her class I saw my true potential: somewhere between the good and the very bottom. I would get very high marks on one test then crash on another. She once commented to me, "Greenstein, you're fast, but you're bad." It was true. I picked up the concepts fine but in my rush to apply them would misplace a decimal point or make other mindless mistakes. I got an 85 in her class. French was a different story. My teacher asked me a question, in French, on the first day in class and I answered in English that I didn't understand. He went on to insult me both in French and in English and picked on me and a few other boys throughout the term. He flirted shamelessly with the girls, touched them on the back of their bras and stared down

Chapter 3. Crossing Tremont

the chests of the few girls that had them. I managed a 65 on the statewide regents and that was what he gave me on my report card. Sometime in that second semester I think I subconsciously gave up on academic achievement.

The only saving grace to my high school years was my English teacher, Mr. Lee in 10th grade. He made us read a book a week on top of all the other work we had, and gave us interesting assignments such as writing descriptive paragraphs without articles. He suggested that we all get personal subscriptions to the New York Times (which he claimed he read cover to cover each day), opened up the world of Shakespeare to me and encouraged us to contribute to class discussions based on our own interests. He was the best teacher I ever had.

I hoped to get Mr. Lee again the following year but was not so fortunate. Instead, I had the mean spirited Mrs. Applebaum. We were all seated alphabetically in her class and by luck of the draw, three Michaels sat behind each other. She would walk slowly about the room, throwing questions aimlessly into the air until she turned on a hidden pivot and called out a student's name. It didn't take long for her to call out "Mike..ll and watch to see who answered. All three of us shrank in our seats until after another interminable silence, she would slowly enunciate a last name. This teasing was cruel and I hated her for it.

One day she announced a special class project. We were all going to read the book *Arrowsmith* by Sinclair Lewis and a few students were going to be picked by her to be on a special panel exploring the themes of the book. She handed out the book, the special theme assignments and called out the names. I could have predicted she would pick me and my heart sunk when I heard my name. Days passed and my anxiety grew. I was paralyzed by fear but there was something else, a growing sense of rebellion. I was determined not to read the book, but I also needed to complete the assignment and avoid embarrassment. Then it hit me. Having mastered library skills in the 7th grade,

I would research everything I needed to know about the book and my theme question. I probably spent more time doing the assignment my way than I ever would have had I read the book. I had my notes organized, memorized key facts and, on the day our presentations were due, I felt as prepared as I was going to be. Not knowing the full story or the characters but knowing the intricacies of 5 to 6 questions, I sat at the table and presented my opus. I was astoundingly good. After my turn, the others on the panel began speaking. I again harbored a fear that I would be asked a question or ask to comment on my fellow panelist's presentation. But I handled this well, drawing upon the bits and pieces of information I picked up in the classroom discussion. Everyone, even Mrs. Applebaum, complimented us for a good job.

The purpose of Science Technique Lab was to give students practical experience in a scientific endeavor. We had to research a scientific idea, conceive of a project, then build and demonstrate it, all in one semester. In other schools, such a class would be called Shop. It amazed me that many kids got to work right away. What were they thinking of? I hadn't a clue where to begin. By the time I came up with an acceptable idea, June, a girl in my class, came up with one that was similar. So, I did the chivalrous thing and let her have the project. But she needed my help to complete it. So I wound up doing her project before I even had another idea to run by my teacher. She wound up with a 90 and I failed for the quarter. This went over real well with my father who screamed, threatened, insulted and glared at me for months. I had lived up to my father's expectations, Mrs. Smith's expectations and my own expectations of failure. Like Freddy had written into my yearbook, I was a doofus in Science clothing.

At some point during the school year I was called down to the guidance office. A middle aged woman with many things on her mind ushered me into a chair in a closet that masqueraded as a workspace.

Chapter 3. Crossing Tremont

"You know why you're here?" she asked. I stared at her blankly, scared and unknowing. Did I set something on fire, I wondered? She held out a copy of my transcript with my "less than Science perfect" grades. They sure looked familiar to me. I said nothing.

"Is everything alright?" she asked in a matter of fact voice. I gave my response the same level of emotional commitment.

"Yes."

A few moments of silence passed. Then, "Have you considered transferring out of Science, to a local high school? You know some of them are quite excellent." I waited a few seconds to give her the impression that I was giving it some thought.

"No," I replied. She turned and went back to the papers on her desk.

"That's all," she said and didn't look up.

Mark

Mark was my friend Gary's older brother. By the time we became friends in Rochdale, Mark was away at college. He seemed to appear at odd times, coming and going on his way to other places. He was very smart and charismatic like Allen, but here the comparison ended. Everything about Mark screamed counter culture. He looked like John Lennon and held radical views on just about everything, or so it seemed to me. He was never without the company of the prettiest, hippest women. One even revealed herself as a witch. I admired his girl friends, admired his freedom and his natural courage. He seemed to be on a relentless journey to find himself. His energy and passion could be overbearing at times and a simple conversation could be taken to ideological extremes.

Mark had left a number of his books behind in the house between journeys. As an avid reader I claimed them. These books introduced me to social and political theory, and encouraged my interest in metaphysics. Ouspensky's The Psychology of Man's Possible Evolution was the right book for me at the right time. Not only did it reinforce the fact that people have been always been struggling to understand their true nature and find their place in the cosmos, but it updated the context and gave Eastern philosophy a more Western tone. This spoke to me more directly and the ideas resonated with my experiences. I had yet to meet a seeker of truth that was not part of a group of smiling people donning strange robes, repeating nonsense syllables. This formulation and introduction to the enigmatic Gurdjieff had well-know historical adherents. As I was to learn, one of the current ones was Mark. Although I knew it was unfair to judge any teaching by one of its followers, I could not help but think that Mark, driven by a compelling need to pursue his studies, was not a model of humility or compassion. I questioned whether he was truly benefiting from the teachings.

The books of Ouspensky and Gurdjieff were an important step for me in a positive yet uncertain direction. The Gurdjieff movement was vibrant and growing while he was alive, but seemed to have lost its vitality in the years since his death. It became clear in my mind that what I needed was not a dying ember to cling to, but a living, ever present teaching. And rather than follow an imperfect example, why not search for a person who has completed the journey, a living exemplar? I knew I was getting closer to something important to my development, but what?

The brush with evil: The old lady on the train

Hy was a deli man at a supermarket in the Bronx. He was quite proud of his skills and he often told me, "Not just anyone can slice smoked salmon." My father knew him for years when he traveled the supermarket scene as

Chapter 3. Crossing Tremont

a sales rep for Breakstone foods. He met up with him at the barbershop in Rochdale Village and he arranged for Hy to drive me to school as he worked nearby. Hy liked to complain about this hardship. I know that if my father had heard him speak this way, Hy would have found himself on his back.

But Hy didn't really drive me to school. He drove directly to work, which left me with a nice little uphill hike on the other side of the reservoir to get to Bronx Science. It wasn't too bad in the spring, but in the winter, a cold wind would blow off the water. No matter what, I would have to schlep around the reservoir to school. It was a small betrayal I bore in silence. One day Hy told me that he had to go to another store for a few days that was just opening to help them get set up. The store was a few train stops away from school, so I didn't mind because I was able to avoid the walk around the reservoir.

The platform and the train were crowded that day. I got near an open door and allowed myself to be pushed into the car along with the other waiting passengers. The ride began as uneventfully as any other until I felt a sharp elbow jab into my ribs. I looked to my side, there was a seemingly innocent old lady. I figured she had lost her balance and toppled into me unexpectedly, righting herself and her sense of balance with her outstretched elbow. She didn't look at me and I figured she was embarrassed, so I let it go and thought nothing of it. A few seconds later I felt a hard pinch on my arm and this time I studied my attacker. She was small, about 5' with a face full of lines, heavy red lipstick and red hair that could only come out of a bottle or from a cheap wig, sticking out of a small hat. She held my eye for a moment and then looked away without expression. I moved away from her as far as I could and noticed that she began to slowly move towards me. The train came to its stop and the person in front of me jumped out of his seat. I quickly sat down before the people standing next to me processed what was happening and I lost sight of my pursuer. "Just another day in NY," I said, to no one in particular, and wouldn't have thought much about it had it not been for events of the next day.

It was a day that promised snow: A yellow-gray cruel sky, the air, crisp and cold. I came prepared with raincoat, hat, gloves, umbrella as well as the usual paper-bagged lunch and book bag. Hy let me off at the same train station and I waited in silence on the station platform. Unlike the day before, just a few passengers were there, and when the train came, they boarded into different cars. I stepped through the opening door and noticed that the car was completely empty. Empty, that is, of people. Strewn newspapers were on the seats, discarded coffee cups on the floor and the walls were screaming with graffiti letting the world know who once occupied the space. I sat down in one of the seats lining the walls of the car and pulled out one of my books to study.

As the train got rolling, the door connecting the cars opened and the same old woman, dressed for the weather with a long coat, hat and flowing scarves, came walking through. She quickly saw me and I thought I sensed an instant look of recognition on her face. To my surprise, she sat down next to me and began shuffling through her old woman things. I didn't expect this, felt somewhat in control of the situation being that we were alone, and was curious at the same time. She became increasingly fidgety and began to move her arms and her legs to get comfortable. Her spasmodic movements brushed my arms and leg. She probably was waiting for my response but I gave none. What I didn't notice was how she positioned her hands under her long scarf that fell off her shoulders. The train came to the next stop and other people came on and took seats scattered throughout the car. As the train started to roll forward, she gave me a long hard pinch on my upper thigh. I winced but said nothing. I realized I had lost control of the situation but also knew that if I yelled out in pain or yelled at this woman to stop in the

Chapter 3. Crossing Tremont

moving train, I would look like an idiot and she might say I that assaulted her. Still she looked straight ahead without looking at me. The bottom of her lip curled in a mock smile. I was afraid and didn't know what to do. Then she pinched me again. Long and hard. My stop was coming in soon and I came up with a quick plan. I waited when the doors opened. They were about to close when I jumped up quickly, jammed the point of my umbrella into the top of her foot with all my might. I felt it break the skin but did not wait to see the damage. I hurried out of the car with the doors slamming. I knew she wouldn't say a word. I turned around and looked at her through the glass. She gave me a wide smile and I understood. She won. I had resorted to violence and become like her.

— 4 —
Reinvention

Dream

I was observing someone put together a life size, three-dimensional jigsaw puzzle of me. Most of the pieces do not fit together. Some are very large and are being shaped down by hand to fit the outline. Other pieces are the right size but these don't fit either. These too are twisted and torn to fit the outline.

Chapter 4. Reinvention

QCC

It was drilled into our heads when we were quite young that we were going to college, to make something of ourselves and take the opportunity that my father never had. It was also clear that we were going to stay at home and go to the free city colleges. There was no other option. But as my high school grades continued to decline, it never occurred to me that I might not qualify for one of the four-year schools. But that's exactly what happened. In those years the city colleges were held in high esteem. Open admission was a few years away. The baby boomers applied and the required average to get in went up. In fact, it was .01 higher than my high school average. I knew of one other kid in my predicament. He argued, begged and pleaded and was admitted into Lehman College in the Bronx. I took my notice of admission to Queensborough Community College as a deserved punishment and kept quiet. It was not easy for a Science graduate to admit going to a community college but I was so glad to get out of Science, and looking forward to a new beginning.

Queensborough was located on a former golf course. The Administration Building was in the Clubhouse and many of the classrooms were in makeshift prefab units. They also rented space in a shopping area a half mile away. This odd layout made it a real challenge to set my class schedule. They were just building up the campus and all the mud and the dust were fine with me. It added a sense of excitement, energy and growth. I liked being there. Compared to Science, the kids were dullards, but I felt I was seeing another side to life. Some of these kids were pretty wealthy and showed it. Many had their own new model cars and drove them regularly to school. Girls paid more attention to their wardrobe and dressed stylishly. Some of the students were just returning to school after serving in the army and were considerably older than I was. There was greater diversity, even for Queens. Only a handful of blacks graduated in my senior year at Science but there were proportionately more in attendance at Queensborough.

My father insisted that I wear a white shirt and tie to school every day. He wanted me to stand out and for the teachers to notice me. Well, he got what he wanted. Everyone noticed and I felt like a fool. After some kids got to know me they would ask me why I did it. I couldn't tell them that even at my age, my life was run by a tyrannical father. It was simply easier to take responsibility for it and say that I wanted to make a good impression. No one bought into this reasoning, but after repeating it a few times, they began to leave me alone.

I had to take a language and I started fresh with German, the nemesis of my brother's college career. I liked it and did well in my class. In fact, in my second term, I was eager to read some of my favorite authors, Hesse, Rilke and Zweig. I went to the library and armed with a dictionary, read the German weekly magazine, Der Stern, and tried my hand at the works of these authors. I also found some German children's books and was surprised how difficult they were for me. I was doing fairly well with my translations but there was only so much time I could devote to this activity. I also had to take a mandatory gym class and took basketball and volleyball. I never played volleyball before and was surprisingly good for a short guy. But I never played a game of basketball in my life and my teacher wasn't about to teach me. On the day we were going to be graded we were assigned to 3 on 3 teams. My team was composed of abject losers like me. The other team was stacked with superstars. It started and ended in a rout but some curious things happened along the way. I stole the ball from one of the jocks twice and although I couldn't dribble more than two steps without turning the ball over, I received catcalls of appreciation from the crowd of students and my teacher. Fifty percent of the final grade was a paper and pencil test on the rules. Most kids took this for granted. I studied up, aced it, and received an "A" in the course.

Two Women

As part of my makeover in QCC, I decided to face my fears and ask out one of the beautiful young women I admired. After a couple of weeks of scouting around, I asked out a girl in my English class who had coffee with me. She flushed, turned red and said that if circumstances were different, she would have enjoyed going out but she had just become engaged two weeks before and her ring was being resized. I didn't know what to say but my experiment with women was over for the moment. I didn't ask another girl out that year.

As the term went on, I became friendly with a tall German girl. We would go over homework, meet for coffee and hang out when we had free time. She was my buddy. Like many others at QCC, she lived a very different life than me. She lived in a private house, was wealthy, had close family ties, was involved in her community, was proud of her heritage and marched every year in the Pulaski Day parade. One day, with a shock of understanding, it occurred to me that she was falling in love with me. She was just waiting for me to notice. And when I did, I couldn't look at her the same way. I felt overwhelmed, intruded upon and not deserving of her feelings. I picked a fight with her, which was not easy, and wound up telling her that I hated all Nazi sympathizers. I knew she did not believe a word I was saying but she got the point that I wanted to hurt her and that was enough. I continued to wonder if I would ever get it right with a woman.

Waking Up to Life

It was an unusually warm spring Sunday. I had loads of work to do for school and didn't want to stay cooped up in my bedroom. So knowing I was apt to be distracted by any and everything, I took a book and went downstairs. I found a bench opposite a tree, sat down and started reading. I wasn't there long when the warmth of the sun, an occasional cool breeze and the noises from passers-by seeped into awareness. I stayed with this feeling, this "being-in-the-moment," and imperceptibly, it filled my consciousness. My sense of self, my boundary with the physical world, dissolved. It was as if a veil had fallen from my eyes and I was now looking upon my environment with an understanding that was intellectual, visceral, emotional, and intuitive, all at the same time. In one moment there was dissolution and what remained was clarity. I sensed the life force of the man passing in front of me, of the tree and of all living things. At that moment I knew something ineffable that I had never known before. Its "rightness" was self evident. This experience was a brush with Truth, a glimpse into the realm of the Divine Intelligence.

And then as incredible as this experience was, it was over and everyday perception returned. I went to the supermarket to find my friend Howie who was working as a stock boy to tell him about it. I didn't know what to say and blurted something about being one with nature. I realized how strange this sounded and I thought he might think that I went off the deep end. I was glad when he didn't have time to talk. The thought entered my head that maybe I was crazy, but the experience was so positive and uplifting, I knew it couldn't be a hallucination. This was something I could not have imagined. It seemed super-real.

For the next several years I found my mission. I wanted to know about this experience and I wanted to experience it again. I relied upon my trusty companions, the library and the bookstore. If I wasn't crazy, others must have had experiences like this. I was determined to find out and it didn't take long. I read Aldous Huxley's accounts of his experiments with hallucinogens, found Burke's marvelous

Chapter 4. Reinvention

Cosmic Consciousness, read of oceanic experiences described by Sigmund Freud and rediscovered Hesse. This was just the beginning. If people wrote books like this, there must be people still having these extra-perceptual experiences. I vowed to seek them out and learn from them.

CCNY

I did well enough at QCC at the end of my first year to transfer to a four-year college and picked CCNY. My brother had gone there and I was a little familiar with the urban campus. It had a better reputation than Queens College, had a more diverse student body, and I was already battle tested from years on public transportation. Besides, I didn't quite relate to the well-heeled student body at QCC. I hoped to link up with some old Bronx cronies and enjoy a better social experience, but this never happened.

Chemistry

I thought I knew a lot of chemistry from high school, or at least I thought I did, having taken chemistry, analytical chemistry and the history and development of science. I had also taken a year of biology at QCC and had done OK, but I was not ready for the introductory science class at City: A big lecture class where the material is presented so fast you don't have time to think and small recitation sections headed up by grad students. So much was presented as fact to be memorized. I wanted to know how these facts were arrived at. I asked question after question of the grad student until he said, "psychology major, right?" And when I nodded, he told me that I couldn't ask another question in class. He said that he would speak with me privately in his office and would give me as much time as I needed. I hated the idea of spending more time on chemistry, but I took him up on it and he was gracious once we were alone.

Lisa, my lab partner was an attractive dark skinned woman from the Dominican Republic. When I asked her out she told me that she was living with her boyfriend, but most definitely would have gone out with me otherwise. These "almosts" meant as much to me as the real thing. Both of us were floundering in class but even with all the help I received after school, I didn't do well on tests. The standardized mid-term was a killer. We had heard that most people did poorly and that grades would be scored along a curve. Our papers were handed out and Lisa grabbed mine out of my hands before I could see it. She burst into laughter and ran around the lab, teasing me mercilessly. My heart sank when I saw the grade, the lowest I had ever received: 19. The passing mark was 35. Lisa refused to tell me what she got until after class I nearly tore her books apart to see her paper. When I finally got my hands on it, she looked at me with the funniest grin on her face: 11.

I continued my one-on-ones with my lab teacher but I feared the final exam. At last, I told my teacher, "If you fail me, I'm going to take this class over again with you." I got a "C" in the course and when I received my grade, stood over a garbage can and ripped out every page in the textbook.

Esther

I first met Esther in my senior year in High School. She was cute, small, Jewish, had brown eyes and hair and was the only girl in the entire school who was engaged so, of course, for me, it was love at first sight. There was no point in speaking to her about my feelings as I wouldn't even know what to say. She was unavailable and I was left to my yearnings and feeling sorry for myself. I did not see

Chapter 4. Reinvention

her for 2 years until my sophomore year in City College. First thing I noticed: No ring. I still felt the undeniable pull of my first attraction to her. She was adorable. There was something here that was more than lustful yearnings. I asked her out on a date and was thrilled when she said yes. I never had a girlfriend and was lost in uncharted territory.

It took me well over an hour, using a bus, two trains and a three visa checkpoints to get to Burnside Avenue in the Bronx from Jamaica, Queens. No matter, I was exhilarated. In my eagerness not to be late I arrived at her apartment building much too early and waited outside before going up. In one of the more amazing coincidences in my life, who should walk by but Harriet, my first heartthrob from Hebrew school. I had not seen her since she was twelve and here she was at twenty one, a beautiful young woman. She was with a gorgeous guy and they were hurrying somewhere. All the old confused feelings of longing and not measuring up came rushing forward. She caught my eye and stopped short. "Harriet," I blurted out. She smiled warmly, spoke my name and asked what I was doing there. "Who's Harriet?" demanded the hunk? I understood at once that I was now talking to Linda. It was her middle name. We made some small talk and Linda asked me what I was doing there. When I told her that I was going on a date she asked why I didn't go upstairs. If I could answer that question, I would be a very different person, perhaps more of the person I wanted to be. A person who felt comfortable with himself and with others. I fumbled some response when the gorgeous guy tugged at her arms to get going. I was too embarrassed to ask Linda for her phone number. I felt overwhelmed with conflicting feelings. Her beauty reduced me to silence. It was like I was back in Hebrew School. I wanted to re-establish some relationship with her, but the promise of Esther beckoned in my mind. I didn't know what I wanted as I watched her walk away, didn't call out to her and never saw her again.

Esther and I went out about every other week for three months. I babysat the other weeks to make money for our dates. I hardly ever spoke to her on the phone during the week. Even though we got on great during our dates, I felt nervous and unsure on the phone and uncomfortable with silences. Nor did we meet at school as our schedules conflicted. Ours was a pretty chaste relationship. There was holding and kissing but not much else. We mostly went to the movies or out to eat. We spent very little time alone when we didn't have an activity planned. Her father was often up reading the paper in the living room when we returned from a date. This clearly bugged Esther and we only retreated to her bedroom. Her mother loved me. If only her daughter felt the same way.

I saved up to go out to a play and night club on New Year's Eve. It was bitterly cold and if I hadn't already spent the money, I would have preferred to do nothing. Still, New Year's was New Year's and I planned to confess my feelings to her, which were pretty obvious by now. Back at the apartment, after a decent date, everything fell apart. Esther saw where my conversation was going and tried to avoid going there. But I couldn't help myself. I told her I was "crazy about her" and she said "don't be." I left the house and cried my way back to Queens.

My relationship with Esther was a one-way affair although I hadn't realized it. I was too unsure of myself and she did not care enough about me. My father, of all people, had sensed this and tried to warn me off, but I couldn't hear such a message, especially from him and especially in his unique manner of delivery. "Dummmp her! She's no good for you. She's a taker! Dump her!" When the inevitable happened he was actually sympathetic. He never saw me so depressed and didn't know what to do. I was in a fugue state, going through the motions of my daily routine without any emotional attachment. I had not only lost someone I loved, I lost what I thought was my only hope for love and acceptance. Howie, trying to console

Chapter 4. Reinvention

me, gave me sound advice. He said, "Don't be a beggar in love." But that was a good description of how I felt. I would have given anything to get back together with her. To go back to exactly the way it was, whether that was the best thing for me or not. With me pining for her, hoping that she would love me and heal me.

A few days afterwards, I was in my bedroom, bent over my grandmother's small vanity mirror on my dresser to check out the latest condition of my temperamental skin. As I gazed into the mirror, to my horror, I saw large sections of my face broken up into oblong swirls of living protoplasm. I stepped back in fright and caught my image in the large dresser mirror and I appeared whole. But I did not have time to react. For I felt something course through my veins, circulating throughout my entire body. I was aware of an intricate flow though it wasn't blood; it was the essence of evil.

When I dared look into the small mirror later that evening, my image remained whole, but the feeling of my evil presence remained. At first it was only a slow sense of movement, almost unobtrusive like a dull headache or minor tooth pain that you can ignore for small periods of time. But the feeling intensified to that of an emanation, like heat radiating off the body after a workout. No longer was the evil merely circulating through me, I now felt that I could spread it to others.

Immediately I realized that I was sick, that my perceptions and feelings were part of a hallucination but this did not stop me from feeling the way I did. I knew I needed help and remembered hearing that a friend of a friend had gone to see a counselor at school. I went to classes the next day and to the administration building counseling office. I was told that I could make an appointment in two weeks. But this could not wait. I insisted on seeing someone right then and was told to wait. After an hour I was ushered into the cramped office of a bored, middle aged man. I had clearly upset his plans for the day and he made it clear that this had better be worthwhile. This was not what I needed. I fidgeted uncomfortably and told him I was unsure about what I wanted in life and searched for signs that I could trust him. He went on a hunt for some papers on his desk, and without looking up, told me to come back in a week and he would give me a series of tests that would help me in the decision making process. I thanked him and left. Clearly, I needed help, but I didn't know where else to look.

Miracle

I went to the train station at 125th Street to take the "D" on the first leg of my trip home. The station was completely deserted. It was eerie. No one on either platform. I went to the edge and leaned over, as I usually did, looking for a sign of an oncoming train. But instead of pulling back and waiting at a safe distance, I lingered, wondering whether I would be better off dead. I stayed that way, leaning, and feeling a peaceful resolve. Lights and then noise. I saw the train approach and stood my ground. Peace. It got closer and I saw the panicked look on the train conductor's face. And then my knees buckled and I fell.

If someone told me this story I would not believe them. How could it be true? How could Moses part the Red Sea? How could Jesus raise the dead? It defied human understanding. Yet what happened to me that day on the train platform did, in fact, happen, and could not be explained by the laws of science.

I was falling and life was again suspended in slow motion, much like my experience in the movie theater so many years before. My eyes locked on the conductor and I saw the terror in his face when I was grabbed violently by the scruff of my neck and heaved upwards and backwards with great force. I landed hard on the platform, several feet away from the speeding train, hitting the back my head as I fell. I was stunned by the blow to my head but bounced to my feet to see who did this, but the platform was as empty as before.

Not a soul was there.

My head hurt but I was glad to be alive. I gave a chuckle and murmured to no one that even in this, I was a failure. My mind wandered back to the time when I had the feelings of closeness with nature. Somehow I felt a connection between the two experiences. If it was not my time to die, then there had to be a purpose to my life, something I was meant to do.

Reconstruction

I reasoned that if I was to continue living then I needed to straighten myself out. I knew that my thinking was distorted and I thought that if could distract myself, I might stop the fears from getting out of control. I knew I could not let despair get the best of me. I sat down at my desk and drew up a battle plan. It helped me to be able to use my intellect rather than focus on my fear.

I knew my household was toxic and that I had to get out if I was to survive. In the short term I had to spend as little time as possible in the house, and in the long term, I needed to get out permanently. But to do this I needed money. So, I had to get a job, save, and move out after college. I went to the school placement office and got a job as a messenger for an insurance company. The following semester, I got a job at the school engineering library. I worked many hours, but still had time for my own studies and made good money at the same time.

I knew that my self esteem was in the toilet. So to help me get a measure of self respect I wanted to learn some new skills to boost my confidence. I decided to learn how to ride a two-wheeler and to ice skate. I rented bikes at a local park and went with my friend Howie to ice rinks. I learned to ride a bike reasonably well for my advanced age of 20 but never felt too comfortable. I gave myself the criterion of going around an ice rink four times without falling. With that accomplished, I called myself a success and never went back to an ice rink again. So far, the distractions seemed to be working.

My grades were ok at this point in my college career, but not great. Part of my battle plan for making progress depended on gaining independence through my education. If I improved my grades I would keep my father off my back and have a shot a grad school. I vowed to study and I did. In my last two years of college, I went straight A.

I still felt heartsick over Esther. But I knew thinking about her constantly wouldn't help my state of mind. I would distract myself, dig into school work, improve my self esteem and hope that she would see the improved me in time and come back. Although this never happened, I ran into Esther several times and I always felt the twinge of longing and disappointment.

Experimental Psych

There was no greater distraction for me than Experimental Psychology. We had to complete a research lab and paper each week. It meant hours of library work, data analysis, report preparation, and typing and retyping the final paper on electric typewriters. There was no way to do this without putting in an all-nighter each week. And this was one of 4 - 5 classes. Choosing a lab partner was hard. I found a real cute girl who told me she only got "A's" and we joined up. Of course, she was engaged but by now I was used to this scenario. She and I became friends throughout our college years and she was a great lab partner. We were the envy of the class and we consistently wrote superb papers. My teacher, who we all thought was a sadist, said that we would one day thank him for all that he did for us. At the time, I seriously doubted it. But several years later I made good on this.

Chapter 4. Reinvention

English

On the first day of class my English teacher stated that he only gave papers, not tests and that he never gave out any "A"s. "A" meant perfection and who in the class could claim to be perfect? For our first assignment, we had to answer some questions about some long boring poem. He wanted our true feelings, but I knew better. I went to the library and researched the topic. Armed with expert ideas, I sprinkled these jewels among my planted grammatical mistakes. The result: "A". This continued for most of the term. Unfortunately for me, the Department decided to give a uniform final exam for all English classes taking this section. When I looked at the questions, I knew I was sunk. We never discussed half of the material on the test and there was no way I was going to ace it. I decided not to take it. I wrote a poem in my little blue booklet describing my opinion that the test sucked and walked out. But I was too frightened to leave it like that. I went to my teacher's office a few days later and sat down with him. He said I was right, the test did suck, but what was he to do with me? The answer was simple to me: With a false bravado I boldly stated that I deserved an "A" based on my work throughout the semester. And that's what I got.

Nick

"Did you read the homework and prepare for today's lab?" Ann asked as she walked in the door, "I haven't the foggiest idea of what to do."

"Well, I read it, but I don't understand it either," I answered, masking my disappointment.

"You know, labs are like...like...some Bergman movie," she exclaimed, peering over her monstrous glasses. "You see it, you to react to it," her hands began moving in circular motions, her voice rising "you like it or you don't. It's impossible not to have an opinion about it, all the while not knowing how you got that opinion, or what you're supposed to do. Don't you agree?"

"I don't know what the hell you're talking about", I stated, "but I can tell you one thing. I don't feel the same sickening pain at the movies that I do right now," I moaned.

"Got a point there. Say, want to go with me to see an old Goddard flick? It just opened around my way."

"Sure." Say, I thought, what's happening here?

"Saturday night?"

"Great."

"About 7:30?"

"I'll be there... Where's there?"

7 P.M. arrived and I was at my destination way too early. I walked around the block three times. My feet started aching and the new shine on my shoes was getting covered by suburban dust. An old woman, perched in her second floor window in an adjoining pre-war building, eyed me suspiciously me on my second round-trip. I avoided her stare. I entered the building and was jarred by the bright light in the hallway, illuminating the long list of tenant names next to the buzzers. I ran down the marquee, skimming the names for the star attraction. I couldn't find it, so I scanned the list again. I recognized that old panicky feeling in the pit of my stomach as the realization grew that I might have made a mistake, that after all my travel and wanderings I might be in the wrong building. "Oh shit. Shit!" I looked around, surprised at hearing my own voice. I took a breath, calmed myself, and walked out of the building. I spied the old hag again. Her interest in me was evident now. I casually looked at my watch. I'm waiting for someone, you witch, I thought to myself, and slowly, I turned around to catch the large name outside –The Edenside– The 400 Building.' Of course, the address of the 400 Building was not related to the street address, but at least it was the one I was looking for. I came back into the lobby determined to come up with a new strategy.

Chapter 4. Reinvention

I looked at the apartment listings that didn't have names; 24A sounded vaguely familiar. I hurriedly ran my finger down the numbers and pressed the black button next to the naked name slot. I was buzzed back. No disembodied intercom voice to check me out.

The door opened. "Oh, hello, Mrs. Applesternenberg? Nice to meet you?" Parents love me so. Why was it so easy to converse with other people's parents?

"Ann's not ready yet? No, I'm not thirsty, thank you." "A fruit? No." "Candy, no thanks, really." "A piece of kugel, just made today you say! Oh I couldn't. But you know, I could go for a cool drink. Seltzer would be fine. No, no ice, thanks."

"Ma, I see you've met Michael," Ann said as she approached from a hallway. I made the quick assessment: Her face was overly made up, probably to cover blotches, but her eyes were bright and alive, heightened by blue liner. She wore contacts and her hair was neatly combed. She had a face and expression I never saw before in school. Where was she keeping it? Gone was the causal camaraderie we shared in lab class. She wore nondescript jeans and a blouse over a turtle-neck. This was a bad sign. They aren't coming off.

"Michael, what luck," she called out as she walked towards me. "My kid sister's boy friend is here, we can double, won't that be fun? And he has a car."

I felt pummeled with a left followed by a sharp right to my ego. Not only weren't we going to be alone but I was put down as second class. I didn't have a car. Being with me and accepting poor middle-class me for who I was, wasn't enough. What was this date all about? Why did she pursue me? She practically begged me to go out with her! Maybe we'll separate from them later? I hoped. Maybe it's not all lost.

But as she neared me my disappointment turned into betrayal. A small fraternity pin lay stuck to her small chest. I wanted to cry but didn't move. Any slightest motion on my part might break the delicate control I had over my emotions. "Oh Michael knows about Pete," she told her mother. I told you about him, didn't I, Michael? See, I told you. Ma." All in one breath. I managed a grunt of sorts and was thankful to have my glass of Tab to focus on. God, I hate that stuff. I suddenly felt that I was in a foreign territory, faking the local customs.

Ann ushered me into her sister's room. The smell of incense clashed with the decor, circa 1940: Lamps with tasseled shades, two large wooden bureaus with inlaid designs painted over white, soiled linoleum on the floor. The absolute jerk who was her kid sister's boyfriend had his back to us, using one of the bureaus as a desk. He did not bother to turn around when we entered. Ann called out to him. "Jim, meet Michael." He turned around slowly, after another 10 seconds or so, obviously finishing the last line in the paragraph he was reading. His expression said it all. We had interrupted his review of the latest edition of Car and Driver. We had done a great wrong. I immediately hated him and turned my attention to Ann's sister. Joy sat in lotus position, with her eyes closed, on her bed. She was wearing a pale blue skirt which had stretched back on her thighs, her entwined legs inviting my eyes to rest upon her panties. She opened her eyes and lifted herself out of the bed to greet me. Very pretty, very young, and very charming.

"O.K. Are we ready to go? asked the jerk.

"And where are we going?" questioned Joy with a look on her face that spoke to a previous disagreement.

"We'll leave it up to Micklelodian, here. What do you say? Will it be the Monster with the Severed Head or The Monster with the Severed Asshole, which will be you, if you don't pick the Monster with the Severed Head." He roared with self satisfaction.

"Jim!" both girls howled at the jerk (my heart was pounding).

Chapter 4. Reinvention

"O.K., O.K. what do you want to do?" he asked to no one in particular, but certainly not to me.

"We can go out, but first let's play the new game Uncle Sidney gave me," Joy quipped. Oh great I thought, can I pretend to get sick and leave?

"Oh please," asked Joy and took the game off her bureau. She looked pleadingly at Ann who stated simply, "It's alright with me. The jerk said, "O.K." and Joy looked inquisitively at me.

"Yeah sure," I resigned. Joy started setting up the game and explained the rules. "The name of the game is Honesty. You pick up a card, read the question and you have to do what it says. After you do it, we read the card and judge whether you gave an honest or sincere answer. If so, you get points and go ahead on the board. If we think you are not honest you go back."

"What do you get if you win," I asked, suddenly aware of Joy's nipples pushing through her cotton blouse.

"Why, nothing," she smiled, "it's just something you do."

As luck would have it I went first. I drew a card reluctantly. ACT LIKE A FISH. I puckered up my face, fish-fashion, and made the most charming "bloobloob" sounds imaginable. Everyone agreed that this was a genuine response and I moved my plastic man ahead three spaces on the board. I looked at Ann, giggling with her sister. Well, at least she is enjoying herself, I thought. I wanted to smear her rouge and wipe my fingers on her sweater. I heard Joy talking to me but I couldn't focus on the words. "Ayy, what's that? I must have been dreaming" I offered.

"The card says that I have to tell the person to my right something personal that I never told anyone before" she explained. She pursed her lips and then bent over to whisper in my ear. I smelled the sweet fragrance of her skin and my arm twitched once, uncontrollably, as her lips brushed against my ear. "My favorite color is red," she said gently.

I pulled away. "I don't believe this" I said incredulously, "this is personal?" "It's true...for me!" she shot back, defiantly.

"No points!" I exclaimed, and Joy sat back down on her knees with a frown on her face. Jerkface had to admit the thing he liked most in the world and got points for his answer, "Cars." Then he left the room to call the movie house to find out the time of the next show. Ann also excused herself to go to the bathroom and Joy and I sat there on the floor looking at each other. My heart started pounding, not knowing what to do next.

"Your turn", she said, even though it wasn't. I drew the next card. It read, "WITHOUT WORDS, EXPRESS HOW YOU FEEL ABOUT SOMEONE IN THE ROOM." I showed Joy the card and millimeter by millimeter bent my head closer to hers. I kissed her gently on the lips sliding my tongue into her mouth. She accepted it passively and then started to thrash it about wildly. Before I could develop this further I heard the Jerk's footsteps approaching and withdrew.

"We've got to leave now if we're going to catch the show," he said, closing the game board. Joy pointed her thumb at me, and stated, "He won," but neither of our companions cared.

We sat boy, girl, girl, boy in the movie. As the lights dimmed I kept rehashing the events of the evening. I could not stop myself from thinking of ways to trip Ann or accidentally push her out into moving traffic once we left the theater. I also wondered how I could lose her and Jerkface and be alone with Joy. I began calculating how much the evening had cost me: pants dry cleaned, new cologne, transportation, movie tickets, popcorn, sodas. Then, as if time suddenly foreshortened, the movie was over. I felt inexplicably drained and more than anything else, wanted to be home in my own bed.

When we got back into the car Jerkface stated that he was hungry and wanted tacos, to which Joy responded

Chapter 4. Reinvention

that she found tacos repulsive but wouldn't mind a pizza. Ann emphatically stated that she was on a diet and wouldn't eat anything no matter where we went. No one bothered to ask my opinion and I didn't offer it. We drove in silence not knowing where Jerk was taking us. Then I began to recognize familiar landmarks. He was taking us back to the girls' apartment building.

"All those who want tacos, stay, the rest get out!" he bellowed. We took our cue and all got out quickly. He took off without a look back or a good night. Well, that's one problem solved, I mused, suddenly thinking that things had turned for the better. One down, one to go. The sisters led the way into the building, tittering between themselves. I glanced up at the window of the old hag. She had finally relinquished her lookout for the night. I returned my thoughts to the task at hand. How was I going to handle this? I searched my mind for a creative idea but found none. I felt a drop of sweat trickle down my armpit as we reached the apartment door. Ann turned to me, said she had a great time, kissed me quickly on the cheek, and slipped into the apartment leaving me behind with Joy. When did they plan this? They went to bathroom together in the movies, I remembered.

"Joy, I was really glad I got to meet you tonight," I began with growing confidence.

"Me, too," Joy replied, matter-of-factly.

"In fact, I'd be glad to see you again, to take you out." I closed in on my target with a half step.

"Why?" came the reply. Oh my God, I thought, this was a real question. Then she folded her arms together and locked them into position on her tummy. What does she want? I really couldn't handle trying to read her signals.

"I don't know," I stated, "maybe it isn't a good idea. Good night," I said a little too loudly and turned to go back to the elevator.

"It was nice meeting you," Joy called back. "Call me some time."

Back on the street I felt released. I wanted to get as far away from the building as possible, to put the evening into the category of bad memories. I walked to the bus stop and kept on going. I passed the next stop and picked up my pace. I felt as if tiny pieces of me were being put back into place with every step. After a half hour my black leather shoes were beginning to feel tight and I found the next bus stop sign and leaned against the pole, finally allowing myself to feel tired. I stared straight ahead not focusing. Slowly I began taking in the street around me. It was quiet everywhere. Small, one family houses closed up for the night. A few with light penetrating through bedroom curtains and shades. Unwavering street lights. No barking dogs. No people. No cars. No buses. I began noticing the smaller details of my new environment. A child's truck left on the lawn to my left, a broken wooden fence picket bent at right angles, with some material clinging to the wood, probably snipped off from an unwary passer-by, mail left in front of the house across the way, a paper in the driveway. The distant backfire of a car spoiled my reverie and I returned to the silence. Still no buses approached.

Things are slower at night, I rationalized. Unthinking, I started circling the Bus kiosk in ever wider arcs. When I reached a radius of ten feet I noticed that the bus route and time schedule were posted on the pole. I walked over slowly, not wanting to face bad news. Christ! The last bus left over an hour ago.

A surreal loneliness crept over me like a shadow. I felt enveloped in the stillness and slowly slumped to the curb as my legs gave way. What am I going to do now? And then behind this, came a flood of blinding anger. Then the tears. In soft, mournful sobs, words came from deep within me: "I hate this evening. I hate the darkness. I hate my life. I hate myself." I stopped crying and blew my nose. I started to laugh when I heard my own foghorn. Maybe someone will think it's a call from a Volunteer Fire Department.

Chapter 4. Reinvention

For the first time I noticed the dark gray clouds moving so quickly and silently through the night air.

The sky looked majestic.

I was filled with awe and humility before the act of creation that was unfolding before me.

Ceaseless change.

Solemn and unspeakable.

And I perceived from an unknown recess within me, an interconnectedness, a sense of purpose in the cosmos, an intuition recalling past experiences with long forgotten memories.

The hardness of the pavement intruded into the moment.

"O.K." I heard myself saying, "This is it, your big chance. It's just me and you here, if you're here at all. You know, I never gave you any credit for existing and now it's time to put up or shut up. If you're out there, get me home!"

I saw headlights a couple of blocks away and stared unbelievingly. The glowing orbs took on a familiar shape as they approached and I recognized the yellow cab with the off duty lights on. False alarm, I mused. But the cab, the only animate object I saw in the past half hour, riveted my attention. My eyes followed it as it slowly advanced and passed by. Then it stopped. It backed up and stopped in the middle of the street in front of where I sat. Still I said nothing.

"Well boy, you gonna sit there all night?" a husky voice called out to me. I looked at my savior in disbelief. Is this an angel sent to me? An answer to my prayer? "Your mamma's gonna be real upset if you don't get your ass home," he said insistently, "now do you want a cab or don't you?" One doesn't look a divinely inspired gift horse in the mouth. I scrambled to my feet and got in the cab.

It smelled bad. Whoever sat there last hadn't washed in weeks. I opened the window to feel the warm air on my face. The images passed by quickly and I enjoyed the kaleidoscope of local colors.

"Hey, where are we going?" I called out, realizing that we were traveling in the same direction from which I had come. I continued, "You didn't ask me where I wanted to go."

"Go? You're going somewhere looking like that? A party maybe? No," he started to chuckle to himself. "You've got to straighten yourself up first."

He pulled into an all night diner and I was mortified that I might meet someone I knew. I followed Nick (I read his name off the license on the front dash) and sat down opposite him in a booth. I took a good look at him and wondered how I had gotten into this predicament. His face looked like he was a veteran of one too many street fights. There as a scar, probably from a knife wound, running across his face from his thick bushy brow down to the bridge of his twice broken nose and onto his cheek. His teeth were crooked and tobacco stained. His black hair was close cut and gray at the temples. Only his eyes, alive and full of light, held forth the promise that he was more than I feared.

"Tell me about yourself," he started. He took a deep drag from a Camel and turned his face to blow the smoke away. When I hesitated, he said, "Alright. I'll tell you." He sat back in the booth. He seemed to exude warmth and smugness at the same time. "You just had a fight with your girlfriend, right? And for some reason, you are afraid to go home...having trouble talking to your folks? So that's it. Your mother or your father?" And after a few seconds of silence, he added, "It's your father, he gives you a hard time, you can't do nothing right. I got it, don't I?" I didn't recognize his expression. Was that a self satisfied smile or was he trying to reach out to me?

"Not too bad," I started in, "but not quite right either." Something about this man invited me to spill my guts. "First, I don't have a girlfriend. I just had a disastrous

Chapter 4. Reinvention

date which I don't want to talk about and yes, my father gives me a hard time."

"What about?" he asked coolly.

"Whatever I do, I can't please him. My grades are not the best, I don't know what I want to do with my life. He says I don't have initiative, he makes me feel like a failure."

"And what do you feel?" he asked.

"I feel like a failure." The words just came out, and as I heard them, tears started to well in my eyes.

"Two coffees here, Joan," Nick yelled out, twisting his compact torso in the direction of the counter, "and a piece of that cake from this morning for my buddy, here." It was enough time for me to regain my composure.

"Thanks," I acknowledged.

"Don't thank me," Nick replied, "You're paying for it." He waited until I was halfway through the stale pound cake before continuing. "So what makes you a failure? Got a criminal record? Sell drugs? Knock some girl up? Forget to get your mother a birthday present? What?"

"I lock horns with him, that's all."

"No, no, you go out of your way to take him on, don't you? You stick it to him, don't you?"

"No!" I said defiantly.

"No," he replied with sarcasm, "when was the last time you went out of your way to do something little for him, or to give in on some small point, or avoid a blow up?"

"You just don't understand, Nick," I pleaded, "He's impossible. And why should I be the one to give in?"

Nick thought for a moment, and then spoke slowly. "What have you achieved with your present course of action? From your own description, you don't seem too happy with your situation. Why not make a change?"

"I never quite thought about it this way," I admitted. "Still, it would hurt," I nearly shouted out the word, "to give in to him."

"Think it would make you less of a person?"

I drank my coffee and picked at the cake. I struggled for a way to prove my point, but my mind went in circles, and I wasn't quite sure what my point really was. I just felt pain in my gut.

There was a long silence and I was happy for it.

"And what have you done for yourself, lately? What plans for life have you made?" Nick continued. "You going to stay in momma's shadow your whole life or are you going to make something of yourself?" I looked at him without saying a word. How much more of this can I take?

There were a lot of valid questions floating around, but no answers.

"What should I do, Nick?" I asked, expecting a lecture.

"How the fuck should I know? Check!" he roared.

Back in the cab he asked me where I lived and we drove the forty-five speeding minutes in silence with the off duty sign on. As we arrived in familiar territory I began thinking about the cab fare. Was he expecting me to pay? How much? Should I give him a big tip? When the cab rolled to a stop, Nick turned around, speaking as if he were continuing a train of thought. "When you start to become more of who you are by doing the things you need to do, you will be greeted with an inner peace. Leave your old man alone. You'll never learn to listen to yourself if all your attention is diverted elsewhere. Now, how much money do you have?" I dug my hand in my pocket and pulled out a twenty and a few loose singles and handed it all to him. Nick took the bills, frowned, and said, "Get the hell out of my cab."

Sideburns

Life at home was better as my stay away tactics proved successful. But it didn't last long. I had longish hair and long sideburns at that time. Nothing short of 1950's duck's ass would please my father. My hair became the latest battle for supremacy of wills. It was the typical "you

Chapter 4. Reinvention

do as I say while you are in my house" scenario. I actually tried to comply and got shorter and shorter haircuts, but ultimately, there was no compromising. Either I cut my sideburns off completely or get out of his house. I really didn't think it would come to that, for my father was sensitive to the opinions of his brothers and sisters. I knew they would never stand for this. But unfortunately for me, he gave way to his own excesses before reason had a chance to work its magic. One day, amid my mother's screams and pleading, he told me to leave. He said that when I returned later, my bags would be packed by the door. I was to take them and leave. I went to my friend Howie's house and his mother told me I could stay as long as I needed to. She advised me not to go home that evening and to let my father cool down. But this did not sit right with me. I wanted to leave on my own terms and I knew that if I stayed away one night, it would be harder to come back on each successive day. I also knew that I couldn't stay at Howie's for long and it would be better for me if I got back into the house and lay claim to my room. I did not think that my father would throw me out bodily and if I just came back, he would have to deal with it.

I came back late at night and no bags were at the door. I went to bed but I knew this conflict was not over. The next day my father reaffirmed a vague statement that I was to leave but I didn't think he had a plan for enforcing his statement. I went to the financial aid office at City College and spoke to a young man who looked only a few years older than me. I explained my situation, told him I needed money and that I wasn't sure where I was going to live. He gave me $10.00 from his own pocket and a bunch of forms to fill out. A few weeks later, when the situation dissolved due to the anticipated family pressure on my father, I received a check in the mail for $150 from the City College Fund and a letter stating that I had been awarded a Tremaine scholarship. I found the young man who helped me and tried to return it. He looked at me as if I were crazy and said that I didn't understand how hard it was for him to get this for me. I couldn't return it. "Take it and use it," he said. I received a check from the City College Fund each semester until I graduated and I have been a contributor to that fund every year since. Meanwhile, my father had stopped talking to me, an unexpected blessing. But he maintained a sense of pride and bragging rights with his sisters that tuitionless City College gave his son a scholarship.

Wake up call

My mental state was definitely improving and I was making progress with my plans for independence but I didn't know how to understand or integrate my recent experiences into the person I was now becoming. One Friday night, for some unusual reason, both my parents had something to do that took them away from the apartment. I was alone and felt myself sinking back to familiar existential questions which had no answers. What was I doing with my life? Would I ever have a girlfriend? Why was I unhappy? It was always the same questions, over and over again in my brain. The permutations seemed endless. I was overwhelmed by emptiness and felt as if I was falling into the actual birth place of despair.

Suddenly, I was on the floor. I don't know how I got there. Like a shock of cold water on a sleeper I was immediately in a different state of awareness. I felt a return to the closeness with the universal force of nature. It was similar to, but more intense than the initial experience I had outside with the trees. The intensity was humbling. I could not press myself any further into the carpet. I felt obliterated, taken out of myself for a few brief moments. I felt enveloped in the sheer power and immensity of the Timeless, the Unchanging, Holy Lifeforce. Then I became aware of the pulse on my neck. It throbbed but

Chapter 4. Reinvention

the feeling of "closeness" was more immediate. Then I returned, feeling an afterglow of good spirits. My rational mind still longed for an understanding that could be put into words of what was happening to me. But, at least for this evening, that longing was stilled with a different kind of knowledge.

Psych 59

One of the better classes I took as a psychology major was Group Dynamics. Not only was this a didactic class, but there were small labs we participated in to observe our own group processes. It was helpful for me to see that the other students were just as screwed up as I was. It was also the only class in which we were instructed not to read the textbook until after the course was over. I was amazed to see how many stages of group experience were played out in textbook fashion. It also happened to be the first class I had in the morning following the draft lottery to determine who was going to Vietnam. Most of the guys, like me, had low numbers and were sure to be drafted. Real life intruded into the classroom and I was glad I was there to share the bonding and caring between people.

I became fascinated with the group process and joined other groups that were offered as part of after class activities. Houseplan Association, the CCNY version of fraternity, announced a Human Relations weekend and I signed up. The experience promised to be intense with many hours of morning and afternoon encounters and it was. At one point in the group a pretty girl, complained of not being loved. I got up from the floor, crossed the room, sat down beside her and put my arm around her. It was liberating for both of us. Later that day, in a large group activity, we were given arts and craft supplies and we were told to express some aspect of our group experience. I made a little clay figure and a larger closed box, symbolic of my inability to express my feelings. The assistant to our group leader, another student who had received training, was paired with me and I had to explain my project to her. She said, "look at that figure, he can't open that box!" I felt the familiar feelings of humiliation start to rise in my stomach. But she took a pencil and smashed the box. It was exactly what I needed. I couldn't have done it myself. Little did I know that nine years later she and I would be married.

Black Student Revolt

In the spring of my junior year, black students protested and took over a building in the North campus. They virtually shut down the college. There were so many issues, from having a Black Studies program, to admissions policies, to racism in society, that I wasn't quite sure what they expected to achieve. One thing was clear, they were angry. I had heard rumors that not all the protesters were students, and some looked a bit older than the students I normally saw around campus. It was a very upsetting time for everyone, including my small crowd of psychology majors. One day a large protest gathering was planned outside the administration building and flanks of police lined the streets, each with a club in hand. As I edged closer to see what was happening, one cop whispered to me to get out of there. He was warning me that something big was going to happen and then I realized that none of the cops were wearing a badge. It was too late for me to escape. Almost on cue, one of the black protesters stepped in the direction of the police and an officer went over to club him. Then all the cops got into the action and the black kids went down quickly. It was brutal but the protest was finally over.

I had long taken an interest in civil rights since the time I drank out of the "Colored-only" water fountain as a little boy. Some of the newer rhetoric frightened me and I feared the consequences that sometimes accompany the

Chapter 4. Reinvention

righting of long-standing wrongs. I had read Rap Brown, Malcolm, Fanon and others. I felt deeply that the rights of all people were tied to the rights of blacks and other minorities. In my heart I felt that none of us would ever be free if any of us were deprived. I saw the black struggle as not too unlike my own. For the most part, I kept my thoughts to myself. Not only would my father have killed me if I became active in a black cause, but I wouldn't have been accepted by the blacks who viewed this as their own struggle. Coincidentally, I was one of the only white students taking one of the first black history courses at the college, appropriately titled, "Black Revolution." It was a mind opener and I learned more about black history and culture than I could have imagined. At the end of the term, teachers across the campus had the option of grading students Pass/Fail. I asked for a grade instead and submitted a paper for my final. When I got a Pass, I went to see the Chairman of the Department. He moved papers around on his desk and hardly looked at me. It was only when I told him what I wanted that he stopped long enough to put a "you've got to be kidding" look on his face. "How would it look," he began slowly, "if the only white student in class received an "A" while all the black students received a "P?"'

"Maybe this white student deserves an A," I replied, with more bravado than I was feeling.

"Maybe so," he said and went back his papers.

Bronx State

I liked my psychology classes, but thought that being a psychologist was probably a lot different than being a college student. I thought it better to find out what a psychologist did while I still had a chance to change my major, then one day find myself in job I didn't like. As my junior year was coming to an end, I wrote letters to hospitals in the metropolitan area asking for a summer job working in mental health. When I didn't get any replies, I accepted a position in a day camp I had worked in the previous year. A week before I was to start, I received a letter from Bronx State Hospital stating they had a position for 6 weeks at $75. I jumped at the chance.

I was nervous coming to work on my first day as any new employee would be. I walked down the hill from the train to the hospital. As I got close, I passed a woman who was walking her dog and thought nothing of it. A few seconds later I heard a sharp, snapping sound on the pavement. The woman had taken off the metal leash from the dog, and was whipping it in my direction, trying to hit me. I started running and so did she, in close pursuit. I ran to the hospital and jumped up the steps into the doorway of the nearest building. I was now inside the asylum, and my would-be attacker sauntered away. It was not the most encouraging start to my new job.

Mr. Foxman, an astute guy in personnel, asked me what classes I had taken in college. When he found out I had taken statistics, he paired me with a psychologist doing research. This humble assignment started my career in mental health administration.

Later on in the day, I was given my first assignment and placed in a small office on a ward. No one had told me what time I was to go to lunch or whether there was a lunchroom. I was introduced to many people, but after a while, I didn't remember who I met and who I didn't. I didn't even know how to get off the ward. Around 12:30, with hunger as my motivation, I ventured about. Everyone was gone and the ward seemed deserted. I felt I might be part of a Twilight Zone episode, "Lost in the mental hospital." Then I heard someone approach. It was a patient who was muttering something under her breath. She seemed to be talking to me but I couldn't make out what she was saying. As she got closer, her voice started to rise and anger flashed on her face. She was now yelling, "Get away from me! Don't touch me!" I was frozen with fear. I saw myself getting fired on the spot. I wouldn't know how to

Chapter 4. Reinvention

explain this to my father. Would he believe me? I retreated and soon had my back to the wall, with the woman still approaching. As she got within a couple of feet of me, I slid away with her continuing to scream straight ahead, this time at the wall. I ran away and felt sheer relief when I found the ward door.

Moshe Vardy was the perfect supervisor for me. He was a good teacher, kind, smart and driven in the pursuit of excellence in his work. He cared for the patients, his students and co-workers. His work ethic was first class. I remember some days he stayed late because he felt he had not accomplished enough that day. I learned more about statistics and experimental design working with Moshe than I had in my college courses. He treated me as a person of intelligence, asked me for my opinion on a whole array of professional matters and, if my thinking was off, would show me where I went astray. I did library research and performed analyses on many diverse issues such as coping skills of concentration camp survivors to changing attitudes of beginning therapists. I helped him publish some papers and he was kind to list me as co-author on one of them. I'm sure he liked me, but the respect he gave me as a human being did more to bolster my self confidence than years of therapy ever could.

As my six week stint was coming to an end, Mr. Foxman found additional funding to keep me on until the end of the summer. Then he spoke to me again in August and told me that an opportunity was likely to develop where I could continue my job in the fall. I reminded him that I was still in college but told him a part-time job with afternoon hours would be great.

Many young professionals came to work at Bronx State and it was surprisingly easy to strike up a conversation and get friendly, unlike City College, where North Campus students came to class and went home. I met Heather who worked as a research assistant for one of the psychiatrists. We had similar jobs and had lunch together from time to time. Like just about everyone, she was at least a few years older than me with the worldly sophistication that comes from living on your own in Manhattan. We were pretty different in many respects. I couldn't wait to go to work. She longed to be at the beach or just about anywhere else but work. She seemed restless for a different life and I was still waiting for mine to begin. By the end of the summer we became work friends and she ran some errands with me after work in her little car. Once she even drove me home to Queens which shocked my parents to no end. I had a feeling that she wanted to see my room, though I didn't have a clue why. We never dated and had no romantic interests in each other.

One day she told me that she had been speaking with Mr. Foxman, and on his advice, had put in an undated letter of leave as she was considering moving to Vermont. At once it hit me. My opportunity for the part-time job rested with Heather leaving! But she wasn't quite sure about what she should she do. She asked for my advice and then surprised me by asking if I wanted to go to Vermont with her.

This question, with the unspoken promise of sexual intimacy, hit me with the force of a train. I couldn't go. I had to finish college. I couldn't drive a car and I had no money. It just wasn't in the script of my life. I told her I couldn't go, which she suspected, and she left for the green hills shortly after. I did get her job, a bittersweet end to a growing friendship.

Bronx State was the perfect complement to City College. While I had lived and gone to school in diverse communities, I never got to appreciate the culture and richness of non-Jewish traditions until I got to know my coworkers. I met people with dreams: professionals who were artists, therapy assistants who were musicians, people from different cultures who shared their food and life, poor women from rich families and really rich people working in public service because they wanted to. I also began a series of friendships with Protestant ministers. Among the patients I met drug addicts, prostitutes and people who committed horrible crimes. I also met four of my life-long friends on the wards. These were the staff, my new extended family.

I Ching

I was convinced that only nuts believed in astrology, tarot, palmistry, tea leaves, and witchcraft. I saw no difference between any of these occult practices, and to me, they were the refuge of the well-intentioned weak. I believed these practices served as a crutch that helped people live their lives. This opinion was not was born out of study of these arts but by observation of the people who professed to get something out of them. Many of these people seemed nice enough when you first met them, but give them some time and they were sure to reveal their true nature or, at best, seem a bit off balance. It's hard to take the advice of a true believer who is chronically depressed or from another practitioner who proclaims undying devotion for silver shoes. Whatever the validity of their beliefs, these devotees didn't seem to derive benefits from them.

I may not have had too many clues about recognizing a real source of Teaching but I knew what didn't feel right. A sure give away was self-righteousness. The knowing smile that says "you're not ready for this yet" or "maybe someday you'll get there." I remember the sadness in one woman's eyes when I could not see the spirits that appeared in her special roll of snapshots. She showed me picture after picture, sure that I would spot at least one of the angelic hosts, but I was not one of the fortunate ones.

I loved to browse through Weiser's Book Store on lower Broadway and was always amazed at the variety of expression of human longing for the divine. I was willing to admit that there may have been some legitimate basis for some people's beliefs at some time in the distant past, but for most arcane material, I felt sure that all connections to real Knowledge were probably lost.

Then I came across Wilhelm's translation of the I Ching with a Foreword by C.G. Jung. Jung, whose ideas were a bridge for me from traditional psychology to a world of growing possibilities, had experimented with the I Ching for many years and had derived great benefit from it. I was willing to give Jung the benefit of doubt but not quite suspend disbelief. I bought the book and took it home. He suggested that the reader approach the book as if speaking with a venerable sage. It was a heavy endorsement and since no one was watching, I decided to give it a try.

But how to make it work? The small appendix, Consulting the Oracle, stated that to tap into the forces which impacted upon my problems and the forces of the universe I needed 50 yarrow stalks or three Chinese bronze coins. As I had neither, I used three pennies. But which side was to be yin and which to be yang? I looked at Abe Lincoln's face but could not get a clue so I went back to the text. Wilhelm said that the side of the coin with the writing was the yin side and the reverse side was yang. As "heads" was usually considered the top, and the reverse side, "tails," I took this for a reasonable substitute. I asked a question: "How can I find spiritual fulfillment?" and I tossed the coins and eagerly wrote down the numbers they represented and the corresponding lines. I looked up the hexagram, Sung/Conflict and was bewildered. What did it mean to "cross the great water?" And who is the being referred to as the "superior man"? The book was either a great fraud or was written in code. I had no idea how this response related to my question. Still, I wasn't ready to give up on it. I needed to penetrate the meanings. I asked the same question again to see if I would get the same answer. This time the hexagram was Meng/Youthful Folly. And I read, "It is not I who seek the young fool; the young fool seeks me." I put the book down. We'll try this another day, I thought to myself.

Chapter 4. Reinvention

My second, third and fourth tries were just as incomprehensible as the first. And then it occurred to me that I may not have been asking the real questions that were on my mind. I was asking "test" questions, looking for profundity when I was not being sincere. I was lonely and in a funk. How could I find a way out? I tossed the coins and received Chun/Difficulty at the Beginning. The Book was telling me to seek helpers and not be passive in my situation. I found this message uplifting and helpful. I didn't care if this was a projection of my own thoughts or something entirely different. I found support and direction I could accept and I didn't feel quite as hopeless. Within a few months I was consulting the oracle frequently and continued to benefit from another way of looking at my problems. At the very least, looking at my life from a new perspective helped keep me moving in the right direction.

The Three Christs of Ypsilianti

My brother once bought a psychology book with the provocative title, *The Three Christs of Ypsilanti*. Ypsilanti was the name of the city and psychiatric hospital which treated three men with the same delusion. What would happen if the three were put together? I never read the book, so I don't know. But what intrigued me was the assumption that none of these three was the real McCoy. How did the psychiatrists and administrators know with a good deal of certainty that they were dealing with a disturbed individual and not the savior of the modern world? I thought this posed an interesting question, but as I was soon to learn, the very disturbed person is always easy to spot. Psychotic delusions are often debilitating. People that have them are not uplifted by them, are not expanded in knowledge or ability, and are generally not fulfilled in their lives. Many find that their ability to function with other people is severely compromised. But the real Christ had once walked among us. How was it that people recognized him? How will modern day Christians know him when he returns? How will the Muslims know him? How will Jews recognize their Messiah? By extension, how would I come to recognize my Teacher?

It occurred to me that while these questions seemed reasonable, their answers lied in another realm. I could not use logic or the powers of reason to come to an understanding of the deeper questions that concerned me. The significant moments in my life were not ones of deduction or the application of intellect but were experiences that expanded my awareness and opened glimpses into a world I never could have imagined. These experiences, whether they were different ways to use the mind or different states of being, were far from the state of mind that formulated these questions. The experience of the great prophets must be something like that. Jesus speaks directly to the open heart. His love, the Messiah's love, my Teacher's love will glisten and radiate from their transformed souls. Will I have an open heart when my moment comes? Will I have the capacity to recognize true spirituality if I ever come across someone so special?

Draft Dodger

My low draft number guaranteed me a visit with Uncle Sam. I got the number of a well known psychiatrist who wrote letters for draft dodgers stating that they were gay, but my self esteem could not handle this deception. I needed another way out. I went down to the War Resister's League office in the East Village dressed up in my usual college attire, a white shirt and tie. I met a long-haired, bedraggled guy in his early twenties, who was straightening up the office and doing some light cleaning. He didn't stop his activities on my account. He looked at me with a mild degree of disbelief and asked me why I was there. It was a simple enough question, but a flood of doubts and uncertainties went through my mind. What if my ideals did not match with the group? How much self disclosure was necessary? Who was this guy, anyway? Maybe the group was a front for Communist agitators. I managed to get my point across in several sentences punctuated with "ummm," "well," "I guess," "ahhh," and other descriptors. He gave me some brochures and invited me to a dinner of like minded people for the following Friday night. I took the number and quickly ran out. I was scared. I felt out of my element of middle class college kids. I didn't feel I belonged in the East Village, with people who looked significantly freakier than I did. I also saw this dinner as an informal interrogation. I didn't want to be questioned about my deeply felt beliefs that I could not articulate. I had to find another way.

I babysat for some interesting people. One man was an English teacher who wrote comedy material for some of the leading stand-up comics. You would never know this by talking with him. Another was a couple that had leftist magazines around their apartment. Somehow, the topic of the draft came up and the wife gave me some helpful advice. The army could not take you out of any medical treatment that they could not provide. They gave me a copy of the appropriate regulations and I began my research. In those days the army did not have any orthodontists, so my post college plan was set. I would get braces. When time came for my army physical exam, I smiled broadly at all the examining physicians. I proudly gave them copies of a letter from my orthodontist stating that I was in treatment for a severe deforming malocclusion and that treatment would last two years. I gave Dr. Norman a copy of my 1-H draft card for his files.

Grad School bound

I enrolled in Experimental Psychology of Learning as I was told that it would look good for my grad school applications. This was the same term as the black student takeover and this class, like many others, was suspended for weeks. A few of us, eager to get a grade (how would a semester of P's look to grad school?), went to see the Professor and asked how we could complete our assignments. He stated that he would give grades to all students who completed their original experiment and paper. I handed in my paper and got an "A" in the course. When I applied to grad school for clinical psychology, I asked this Professor for a recommendation. He was somewhat reluctant and I chalked it up to the shortened semester or perhaps because he didn't get to know me well. But this was a heavy duty course and I pressed him to do it and he finally agreed.

I took the Graduate Record Exam for psychology and thought I was doing pretty well until three quarters of the way through I began thinking of the importance of this test. How my whole college career could be swayed by a really good or bad grade. How it made a difference between just a good school and a really good school. I peered down at my answer sheet and realized to my horror that about 20 questions back I skipped a line on the answer sheet. I had to erase each answer individually and re-blacken the correct spot on the sheet. After I did this I became a bit light headed. The questions became blurry and I had difficulty focusing. I waited a few minutes for this to pass, but felt pressured for time. Disgusted with the system and with myself, I walked out. I got a 660 on the exam which, while not great, was respectable. I applied to several grad schools and waited eagerly for responses. One by one they came in: rejection after rejection.

By chance, a few days later, I met my Experimental Psych teacher walking on the street on the West Side of Manhattan. He asked me how I did with grad school and I told him.

"I'm not surprised," he said matter-of-factly, "maybe it had something to do with what I wrote on your letter of recommendation." I was stunned.

Chapter 4. Reinvention

"What did you write?" I asked.

"Oh, I wrote that your paper was the best I'd ever seen for an undergraduate. I didn't believe you did it." You could have knocked me over with a feather. I called him a son-of-a bitch, walked away slowly and wondered if I could ever undo the damage.

When I was back at school I spoke with one of my professors who I knew liked me. He was shocked and appalled when I explained the situation and that confirmation was all I wanted. But he wasn't going to let this lie. He told me that he would get back to me within a couple of days and I feared that this whole thing would be turned around and that I would be the subject of an investigation. But that's not what happened. He told me that he had discussed the issue with the Department Chairman and they were prepared to offer me admission to their Master's program or Ph.D. program in developmental psychology or experimental cognition. I had my heart set on clinical work and I wanted to get away from the professor who inflicted this damage and the Department of Psychology. I refused their offer, enrolled in the Master's program at the New School and skipped graduation. As I never earned a Ph.D., it was a decision I thought about in subsequent years.

— 5 —
Rebirth

Dream

I was sitting in a meeting at work. A bunch of people were sitting around a table talking. I noticed a strange movement coming from the back of the room. There was a large area on the floor which was covered by peat moss. Something in it was moving. I was scared but approached it. I looked more closely at the dark, moving earth. It was only the occasional movement which allowed me to discern the outline of what remained of a live but decomposing body. It looked dreadful. Parts were falling off. It was me.

Dream

I was in the middle of some cops and robbers scene with people shooting at each other in a crowded street. Someone near me was hit and bleeding. I started running away and ducked into a doorway to hide. It was a nursing home. I stepped into a large dayroom where the frail elderly were sitting around idly. I heard someone say to me: "Some people don't know how to die."

Chapter 5. Rebirth

Back to the future

With money in the bank, a full time job at the hospital, and enrolled in evening classes at grad school, I moved back to the Bronx to a converted basement apartment in a small house in a quiet Italian neighborhood. My salary, at $185 a week was more than enough to cover the $85 monthly rent. I gave myself the luxury of $30 in pocket money per week and for several months didn't even know how to spend it.

    I enrolled in driving school and met Luis, an impassioned Latino whose skills as teacher consisted of growling at me in Spanish. A member of the "neo-realist" school, his teaching method was to bark commands like "drive" and "turn here." But most of Luis's attention was devoted to other drivers. If he wasn't shamelessly flirting, he was cursing and gesticulating with his body half out of the open passenger window. I always took him seriously as he kept a gun underneath his seat. "You never know who you are going to meet out there," he'd say to me with a smile. After eight lessons I took the driving test but failed four times. On my fifth try, Luis tried to bribe the inspectors and told me that if I didn't pass he would lose his job. Somehow I passed.

    School and work kept me pretty busy. I loved being on my own but was unprepared for the long stretches of loneliness. There could be many days in which I did not talk to a soul outside of work and, if I had no plans, weekends could be deadly. My friend Rick had long ago relocated to Minnesota, Gary was pursuing his Ph.D. in Virginia and Howie was still in Rochdale but was dating his wife-to-be. I needed new friends and activities. I liked to cook and began experimenting. I taught myself how to make candles and took a pottery course in the East Village. I wrote poetry and most importantly, began to make friends with the staff in the hospital and with other graduate students.

    One day, the ward secretary, whose office was next to mine, chided me that my socks didn't match. "You're never going to get any dates looking like that," she exclaimed matter-of-factly. "If you can't dress yourself, I'll do it for you. I'll spend your money." I took her up on it. She took me shopping to Macy's department store and selected 2 outfits, slacks and shirts, which I tried on before her approving eye. It didn't get me any dates, but Diane and I became friends for life. The person in the office next to hers was a social worker, an odd ball character who lived in a too-poor neighborhood, taught his cat to attack strangers who tried to pet him and drove a Citroen with the finest leather seats. He introduced me to the wonders of the West Side, Cuban food, and small communities outside the city. Leon and I became fast friends and pool competitors.

By the time New Year's rolled around, I began getting depressed. No date even remotely on the horizon. At the last minute, I called up a friend on the hope that I might find someone to share a beer with and found, to my surprise, that he had no plans. I asked him over. Then, not wanting to be with just him the whole evening, I asked someone else, then someone else, then someone else. Thus began a ritual of last minute New Year's parties which I held for many years. I was finally beginning to carve a niche for myself and feel more comfortable in my own skin.

New School

The New School was not a friendly place. Most of the first year classes were held in a large auditorium. Professors were distant and guarded by their body guards, also known as graduate assistants, who met with students, answered questions, handed out grades and protected their sanctity. Some of the students were clearly aggressive in their pursuit of grades. They sidled up to the young teaching assistants and made appointments to speak with the professors just to keep their name and face prominent. I

Chapter 5. Rebirth

spent much valuable energy hating them but they were hard to avoid.

The New School did not seem to be a place of learning. They took in many new students, charged the going exorbitant fees, and made it difficult for students to graduate by utilizing a nine point grading system ranging from A+ to C-. With the average score in many classes a B- and very few people getting A's, it became extremely difficult for many students to get the B average needed to graduate.

Statistics was a mandatory subject as was experimental psychology. I bought the stat textbook and was soundly disappointed with its simplicity. I knew from all that I learned from practical experience in Bronx State that I could master this material. I did not take the course but studied a couple of weeks before the final and passed. Experimental psych was likewise a joke. The course was baby work compared to my classes at City College. I told my teacher that I was working on research at Bronx State thinking that he would cut me some slack. But instead, he held me to a higher standard. I had to do extra papers and cut back on my participation in class. I resented the treatment, told him so, and he let me know what he thought of me by grading me lower than I deserved. In my second year, I was able to take courses with smaller class sizes but I still found it hard to bond with the professors. I had the distinct feeling that teaching was a secondary interest to most and that they would much rather be somewhere else.

I met Beth at the New School. She was nine years older than me, which made her an "older woman" at 32. She was recently divorced, sophisticated and knew the finest bakeries and cleanest rest rooms in every part of the city. She went out with men who could afford to take her out nicely. Most were older, established and some were married. Beth was a master of her own sexual charm and attractiveness. I knew she was out of my league but my attraction was too strong. She seemed genuinely interested in me, in a non-sexual, non-threatening way and we became school friends. Then, to my surprise, on her suggestion, we began to hang out together when she had no plans. On the rare occasion when I had something planned, I would change my plans to be with her.

About a year into our friendship, I began wondering what Beth's interest was in me and steered a conversation in this direction. I was shocked when she said that all of her relationships with men were sexual but she couldn't talk to them. She found it easy to talk to me and said that she felt free and unthreatened with me. She said that she had often thought about having sex with me but knew that once we did, the relationship would be changed. But everything did change at the moment she spoke those words. The knowledge that this vibrant, sexy woman thought about having sex with me was a tonic to my self esteem. It was almost as good as sex itself. For the promise of real sex would have raised more self doubts and anxieties. In as much as I would not admit it to myself, this was as close to Beth as I wanted to get.

I took nine credits a semester in the evenings for two years. This program nearly killed any interest I had in psychology but by the end of the two years I got my Master's degree and considered myself lucky to have survived the program. I applied to various doctoral programs in clinical psychology over the next two years but didn't get in. I had no doubts that I could succeed in any doctoral program in psychology but I began to think that I might never be admitted.

First Encounter

I walked into a staff meeting late from lunch. I don't remember why I was late that day but I didn't want to risk being later than I was with the big brass present. I felt self conscious carrying my assorted papers and books that I

Chapter 5. Rebirth

wished that I had taken the time to shove back in my office. As I opened the door, the speaker stopped talking and all eyes were focused on me, the miscreant. I felt chastised for my lack of etiquette. As usual, the chairs were arranged in a large circle. I had to walk across the room to the far side, to take the only available chair. To make matters worse, I fumbled with my papers as I tried to gently place them underneath the seat. The thud was loud enough to cause the speaker to turn his head in my direction. Having doled out as much punishment with his glance as was possible, the speaker continued with his presentation. I felt my face redden and sat more quietly than I usually did at those meetings trying not to draw any more attention.

As the meeting was breaking up, Dr. Sam came over to me. Pompous, know-it-all, Dr. Medicine. The doctor with a drug cocktail for any psychiatric ailment. The doctor with the authoritative opinion about treatment. So what that his insights were usually right on target? So what that he usually reported stunning successes with the most difficult patients? His pharmaceutical mind denied humanistic values, or so I thought.

"What do you have there?" he queried, gesturing to the disheveled mess under my chair.

"Just my things," I responded nonchalantly, trying to end the conversation before it began, as I bent down to pick up the items that proclaimed my lateness.

"No, I mean that book," as he pointed to a book on Gurdjieff's teachings. "Is it yours, are you reading it?"

"Yeah," I answered, thinking to myself, "Why is this guy talking to me?"

"Come to my office in an hour and we'll talk about it."

My heart raced with fear. From my readings on cults and mind altering drugs I knew scores of ideologues who were hospitalized after their experience with Scientology, or from LSD. What did this straight-laced guy want to talk to me about? If I told him that I was interested in metaphysical ideas, he would think I was a misguided idiot.

Worst of all, he would lecture me about the true path that only he and a select few knew, and because of his position in the hospital, I would have to sit through it. Perhaps I'd even have to tell him how helpful he was. But I did not want to be impolite and besides, why risk antagonizing him? I resolved to visit his office and try to find out about his motives.

I knocked at his door, and was ushered in. I sat in the chair next to his desk. Sam was smoking a pipe and the smoke drifted out of his mouth and hung about his face like a low cloud, obscuring his features. I felt more at ease, not being able to see him clearly. I became aware that we were sitting there not talking. I can play this chess game, I thought. He invited me here, let him start this.

"What are you looking for?" he asked softly.

Something was different. Already this was not what I expected. This was not the voice of a self satisfied expert, trying to flaunt superior knowledge, debating skills or a potential adversary looking for inconsistencies in argument. This was the voice of someone who was reaching out to me. There was sympathy in the voice and I was taken aback. I felt my attitude instantly transform and I immediately decided to take the risk and speak openly with him. I didn't know what I was going to say. I listened to my words come out as if I were hearing them for the first time. I told him that I had what I felt was a transcendental experience: One day, four years earlier, I was sitting under some trees in my apartment complex when suddenly, without warning, without the benefit of imagination or thought I felt overwhelmed by a state of being that was completely foreign to my consciousness. It was an intuitive knowledge, directly experienced. A part of me shared something intimate, basic and primal with other living things, the grass, the trees, other people. What I was looking for, getting back to his question, was to experience this again.

It was out...I was glad I said it, but my fear instantly returned. I knew he was going to refer me to one of his psychiatrist friends. Maybe he was trying to drum up his own private practice.

"No. You are not crazy," he started. "You will find what you are looking for, and more." And he laughed a laugh I would grow to love in the coming years. "Let me tell you a story," he continued, and he told me a tale about a young man who was in despair who went to the railroad tracks to end his life. It was me, complete in every important detail. But I had never told a soul about this. I sat there dumbstruck, not knowing what to think.

"Do you know why you didn't die then?" he barely whispered. I couldn't respond. "You have work to do." Deep down I had begun to believe my life must have had a higher purpose, but to hear it from a stranger was frightening.

Second Impressions

I stayed as far away from Sam as I could. I was dazed and bewildered by my visit with him. I didn't know how to make sense out of what happened. I felt exposed, bare, and vulnerable. How could he know such intimate details about my life and state them with such certainty? Yet he spoke with calm, unthreatening reassurance. These were some of my most hurtful moments and he spoke about them with caring and without critical judgment.

I also felt excited. Here was person who seemed to understand my experiences, accept them and hold out a hint that more was to follow. Although he said little about my longings, he confirmed them in a strange, understated way. What did he mean when he said I had work to do? How did he make me feel comfortable, even willing, to share such private desires and memories? How did he speak with the confidence of someone who knows? Something had happened in those brief moments that was clearly way over my head.

I reminded myself that under his smiling demeanor was the same person I didn't like prior to my visit. Here was a magician of some sorts. Perhaps he was crazier than me, or a power driven fanatic who wanted to bring me under his influence. Would he use his knowledge about me to control or embarrass me in some way? I was definitely afraid, and not too eager to see him again.

Next Visits

Working on the same unit I couldn't avoid him for long, and again, I was the recipient of another invitation to come to his office and chat. "Bring your lunch. See you at 12." He said and didn't wait for a reply.

I came on time, not sure of why I was there, and sat across from his desk. I took out my sandwich and apple and started eating, waiting for him to make the first move.

"Coffee? Tea?" He was clearly happy to see me and his smile was warm and welcoming. What was I doing there? I kept thinking to myself.

"Coffee would be fine," I replied.

What was it about this simple act of Sam's making instant coffee that gave it a degree of recognizable specialness? Was it Sam's care and attention that went into the mechanical motions? Was it his understated concentration which implied that no business in the universe was to be conducted until this very important act was completed? Over the years I would watch Sam make me coffee and tea and this ritual would take on new meanings for me. Every act, including this one, held within it the personality and substance of the man. Although I could not put words to it at the time, even this simple act held within it a demonstration of his humility and service.

The dance had begun. Simple conversation appeared to have subtle undertones. Sam asked innocuous, open ended questions, leaving a door open for me to tell him what was on my mind. He managed not to reveal much of himself at all. I explored every word of his for evidence of a personality cult or worse, looking to discredit him as

Chapter 5. Rebirth

a charlatan. But after a period of the smallest small talk, I found myself relaxing, much to my surprise, having no reason to maintain my wall of suspicion. Perhaps sensing my change in attitude, Sam asked me about my experiences on the path and my beliefs in God, Truth, the Supreme Being. "Fill in the blank," he said, with a twinkle in his smile. I replied in the negative to all the appellations. God, the Judeo-Christian invention, had no meaning for me. True, I felt pulled in many different directions. I felt a seductive closeness to Jesus. I was attracted to Zen writings, especially Alan Watts. I was enamored by my current readings into Krishnamurti. I had begun readings into the Zohar and the Apocrypha. I had quotes from the Upanishads on my refrigerator. I longed to know the secrets of the Gurdjieff movement but was afraid of its secretive ways. But did I believe in anything? No. Everywhere I looked there seemed to be unkept promises and beautiful words whose meanings escaped me. There was no God, no creator, no master of my fate. I simply was. People, circumstances and things just happen, but that is what makes life so interesting. "We are all in existential crisis," I told him.

Sam really liked this. He stated that he respected a person who didn't sit on the fence and had an opinion. But he wondered, had I given any thought to the pattern of going to sleep at night and my getting up the next day. When I go to sleep, where did "I" go? (Huh?)

And, did I ever give any thought to the possibility that I might not get up the next day? Wasn't the fact that I hadn't thought about this an unexamined belief in my own continuity? That idea got me thinking. For a person who claims not to have faith, didn't I make plans every day with the assumed belief that I would wake up the next day?

The Prayer: I

"So, you don't believe in God?"

"No."

"Good. And you're sure about that?"

"Yeah."

"Then you wouldn't mind trying a little experiment? It won't hurt you I assure you."

"What kind of experiment?" So this was it, I mused, the moment I was waiting for. He was about to show his true colors as a high priest. Would it be the donning of robes, chanting in Urdu or the burning of incense? What weird thing did he have in mind?

"I would like you to say a short prayer two times a day, when you wake up in the morning and when you go to sleep at night."

"No."

"Why not?"

"There is no need to pray. I won't pray to a God that doesn't exist."

"But how can it hurt you? You don't believe in God."

"I'll feel stupid."

"But who will know?"

Well, I thought, I will and he will, but he won't think I'm stupid. He'll think I'm falling into his clutches. But how could it hurt me to say a few words? "How long is it?"

"Four sentences."

"I guess I could say that. What is it?"

He wrote it out on a pad from one of the drug company promotions. He handed it to me and asked me to read it aloud.

I stared at the piece of paper. The words were charged and invasive. I was being asked to make declarative statements about myself which I knew to be untrue. I felt intruded upon as if the foundation of my character was under attack. I felt angry and tricked. It was one thing to say something privately to myself, but by saying these words out loud I felt I was proclaiming something to the world and to Sam, something which seemed so revolting

Chapter 5. Rebirth

and hurtful to my sense of self. Two of the sentences contained the phrases, "I am thy humble servant..." and, "I surrender my will to thy divine will." I couldn't say them. The words stung and elicited strong denial. It was as if I was asked to shout in a crowd of Jews: "Hitler was a great man!"

Sam made me a bet. He asked me to try it out for a month or so. If nothing happened, no harm done. But he predicted that there would be positive changes and these would be apparent to me. The first changes would be external. People would start telling me that they felt better from talking to me or that I lifted their spirits. The second would be internal. What did he mean by this?

"If I tell you, you'll say that it was the power of suggestion. No, you will tell me. In fact, I don't want you to take anything I say at face value. Test it against your own experience."

I Take up the Bet

Why did I take him up on his "bet?" Because it would be a sure thing. Even if he was clever enough to manipulate the events between us, he certainly could not control events outside of the office. I felt I had him where I wanted him. I wanted "experience" and he promised it would follow. I was sure that nothing was going to happen, yet I was excited by the possibility that something might.

I put my little prayer near my bedside to serve as a reminder and started my new ritual. At first, I said the words as disdainfully as I could, and left out the offensive parts, but soon I could not sustain this level of emotion. Disdain passed into vacuity and within a few days I realized that the prayer was memorized. From time to time it would waft into my consciousness during the day. I found it annoying but paid no attention to it.

One day I received a call from a cousin that I had not spoken to in years. Although we were close as kids when growing up, family wars had kept us apart. Out of the blue she wanted to get together. I looked forward to the visit. It wasn't a long one, but I brought a peace offering of rugulach and the ice between the families had been broken. My uncle had been sick and even my short stay tired him. After exchanging pleasantries, catching up on gossip, and glomming pastries, I left satisfied. I thought no more about this until my aunt phoned me several days later. She told me that unbeknownst to me, her daughter, my cousin, had suffered from a terrible depression brought on by her own illness and a failed relationship.

"I don't know what magic you're spinning," my aunt remarked, "but your visit completely transformed her. She's a new person."

That's one, I thought to myself, but it's probably a coincidence.

But I couldn't get this event out of my mind. Sam said this would happen and it did. I wanted more and it came within the week. Both a colleague at work and a friend who had known me for years remarked that I had changed for the better. I wasn't depressed and I appeared light-hearted and happier.

A few days later I sheepishly walked into Sam's office and announced my defeat. Something was going on. I fully expected him to exalt in his triumph. Instead, he remarked casually that this was only the beginning.

"Wait and see."

The Straight Path

Every now and then I would have lunch with Sam in his office. In the beginning, he did the asking. Later on, I initiated the visits. We would sit around his desk eating and talking. I began to loosen up and feel comfortable when, after repeated exposure to him, my worst fears about him were never realized. I saw how he spoke to his colleagues and spoke about his patients and was impressed by the

Chapter 5. Rebirth

fact that he knew them all so well and cared for them. I marveled at the respect his staff freely gave him. This was a man I had misjudged. But who was he really?

I followed my instinct and asked.

"A servant of God," was all he would say.

"But what is that?" He laughed, took another puff on his pipe, and shook his head gently from side to side without elaborating. In all the years I've known him he never referred to himself in any other way. My feelings toward him turned positive, friendly, sometimes reverential, and other times deferential.

As I got to know him, Sam told me a little about his past. He said that he had researched and experimented with many metaphysical systems.

"I studied astrology and numerology, I stood on my head, I bathed in ice water"...his list of adventures made me howl. "This, what I speak to you about, this is the straight path."

"There is only one God and all the religions are like suitors after the same girl. All extol the virtues of the beloved. Some remark about her hair, some her smooth complexion, others her eyes. It is all the same girl. Each of the major religions had a time in which its message was operant. The core of all religions is the same. This is the Teaching and it has always existed."

I looked forward to the times when Sam would talk plainly. Whether I understood what he was saying or not, agreed with him or not, I felt that it was at these times that something important was happening. Learning was taking place at an accelerated pace and I was participating in some ancient custom, in the passing on of Knowledge.

Reading: I

Sam was always interested in what I was reading. I did not have much time for this leisure activity as I worked full time during the day and went to graduate school at night.

I did manage to sneak in a spy book here and there, but I saved these mostly for vacations. He asked if I would be interested in reading a slender book relevant to our discussions. A slender book? Why not?

If Sam had told me I would be doing a lot of reading I would have rebelled. Reading was the last thing I wanted to do. I longed for dazzling, mystical experiences, visions and revelations. I had been reading all my life. There couldn't be anything more mundane to me.

The first book I read was *The Teachers of Gurdjieff* by Raphael Lefort. This was a book about a guy who searches for the teachers of his deceased teacher, and like Dorothy in The Wizard of Oz, is told to go home where he can find what he is looking for. Sam explained that Gurdjieff was given authority for a limited time to introduce some concepts into Western culture. When he died his followers tried to keep his activities alive, but their efforts deteriorated into a cult movement that lost its sustaining influence. I asked Sam if it were possible to pick up the best threads of Gurdjieff's teaching and add it to the best of the other traditions which likewise had attracted me. Sam explained that it might be possible to take two wheels from a Mack truck, two others from a buggy, an engine from a race car, a chassis from a Model T, and put it all together. It might have all the right components, might even look like a car, but constructed in this manner, it wouldn't go anywhere."

I formed a mental image of this car and chuckled. I found this reasoning very satisfying. It explained why so many of many of my friends and acquaintances seemed to be making no or little progress. It seemed clear to me that I needed to stay the course, if only I knew what that was.

— 6 —
Taking Hold

Dream

I am standing somewhere in a featureless plain.

I become aware of a presence, an impending sense of doom.

I scan the surroundings and see a short, balding man standing motionless, about 50 yards away. He has a wide forehead, his right eye disfigured, almost popping out of his head, looking askew. Instinctively I know this is the Antichrist. I am becoming overwhelmed by a pervasive feeling of dread. The intensity makes me turn away. I cannot look at him directly.

I felt that some influence of evil was going to manifest itself. I began to shout, "Allah, I seek refuge to thee from the accursed devil." As I started saying these words, my tongue began to swell enormously in my mouth. I could not make anything but the grossest sounds. I then thought: at least I have my mind, and began repeating the prayer silently to myself.

I awoke. My tongue was swollen, filling up my mouth.

Chapter 6. Taking Hold

The Prayer: II

For no reason at all, I found myself saying the prayer at odd times during the day and I became concerned. First I thought that Sam might have put me under a magic spell. Whatever was happening mystified me. I was going through some important change and although deep down in my heart I sensed this was what I had been waiting for, I was afraid.

"What's happening, Sam?" And I told him what was going on.

"This prayer operates in much the same way as a radio or television. We are continuously bombarded with waves, radio waves, all kinds of waves. This prayer tunes you to pick up the positive vibrations. It attracts the light and dispels bad influences. From now onward your life will change." He lifted his hand and eyes to the heavens and smiled.

Out West

A few months after I met Sam, I came by one day to tell him that I was off for five weeks on a cross-country trip. He seemed a bit annoyed but said, "Don't worry you'll be protected." I hadn't the foggiest notion of what he was talking about. Why did I need protection? From what? And how was I going to be protected, by him? He didn't answer. Still I looked forward to my upcoming adventure and I tried to keep Sam's warning out of my head.

Three guys in a VW Beetle, each with $200 or less in his pocket. These were the days when gas cost $.38 a gallon and you could still find plenty of two dollar black jack tables in Las Vegas. Despite the occasional claustrophobic moments, we had a great time sightseeing, meeting people and camping out. We called ourselves the Merry Pranksters and kept a small journal of our adventures. One day in the southwest my buddies and I stopped off at diner to get some lunch. I was at the pick-up counter and was getting sandwiches. I began chatting with the pretty girl who was waiting on me but I found my attention diverted to a middle-aged Native American man behind the counter. He met my gaze and held it and I felt that, in some way, we had recognized each other. To my surprise, he came over to where I was sitting and told the girl to get behind him. He then told me to leave! The girl was astounded by his rudeness and told him so. I told him that I had placed an order and would leave as soon as it came out. I thought he was annoyed that I was talking to the girl, I certainly wasn't looking for any trouble, but there was definitely something else. He looked at me without speaking for a long while. Finally, he told the girl to check on my order. She brought it out and he placed it in front of me. No money, he said. Just go. This astounded the girl even more. I began to piece the sequence of events together. Whatever he recognized in me, he didn't like. I told him that it was important for me to pay and that if he wanted, he could give the money to charity. He nodded. I paid and, while I was making my way to the door, he said to the girl in a voice loud enough for me to hear that I was a "brujo," an evil witch doctor. I was bewildered. How could he get things so wrong? I thought of Sam's words that I would be protected and left.

Reaching California became very important to me as we trekked our way from state to state. I felt something was waiting for me there. I hoped to find the answers to the important questions in my life. What was I to do? Was there a purpose to my life? How was I to understand the strange but compelling spirituality I found on the ward of the psychiatric hospital?

I hooked up with the brother of a friend of mine. Against my protestations, he dragged me to a church service. Only this was no ordinary service. This was a foot-stomping, rock and multimedia extravaganza. The congregants came from all walks of life. There were street people and the relatively well-off. I was dazzled by the glitz but

Chapter 6. Taking Hold

when the minister spoke, I knew why everyone was there. He was a passionate and sincere man who spoke from the heart. He spoke of the need to keep hope in our lives and the need for all of us to reach out and help our brothers and sisters, especially those gripped by despair. He had that special quality to reach each person as if he was talking only to them. At the end of the service, he embraced each one of us. I felt humbled by his ability to reach out to all of us, me in particular. As I returned his embrace, I found myself saying, "I believe, father." "I know you do," he replied.

As the time was coming close to plan our return trip we had one last day to frolic in the waves of the Pacific. Waist deep in the water, I stared out onto the vast horizon. I realized I had nothing in front of me but thousands of miles of water. To my back, was everything I knew. I had no girlfriend, no career to speak of, no plans for the future, and I wasn't close to my family. Why not stay where I was in California? What was I returning to? And then I knew. I needed to explore what I had started with Sam. I needed to see this through.

I told all of this to Sam when I came back. He chuckled and said nothing.

A Question of Faith

How do I know if God exists?

This is a question asked by millions for countless years. A question I now asked with a new degree of earnestness. I had moved from being a disbeliever to a fence sitter, from a state of surety to anxiety. I was at a turning point which would determine my future direction and did not know how to proceed. I thought of Sam's calmness and confidence, how he always seemed to have an answer to every question whether he choose to tell me or not. Although I regarded him as knowledgeable, extremely bright, special in a way I didn't understand, charismatic, and at times, enigmatic, I came to realize that Sam's answers could not satisfy me. I could not turn to him or another human being to know about God. Nothing would satisfy me short of my own experience.

If there was a God, who would know? And then it hit me. God would know. And if there was a God, as I conceived of God, God would know of my struggles to know. I felt invigorated with this thought and I remembered a passage from the Old Testament where Jacob struggled with an angel and would not let him go until he received a blessing. I felt that this must be my course and began to think of God as my companion that I would not let go. I would talk to him. I would appeal to him. I would be a nudge. And I would learn to listen, if there was anything to hear.

Change

Almost a year after I my conversation with Sam in his office I realized a profound change had taken place. I knew it the moment I woke up. I was different. A cloud that lay upon my consciousness, one that I did not know existed, had lifted. I felt freer, content, even unrestrained. It was unmistakable. It wasn't a feeling of elation or a moment of happiness or a change in mood. I knew in the very nature of my being that this wasn't transitory. I experienced myself differently. I was the same person, yet inwardly, I was an improved version of myself. Calmer, clearer and at peace. I remembered reading analogies from other traditions which likened spiritual growth to peeling away the layers of the soul like an onion. I felt one layer lighter.

I was astonished. I knew that in my "normal" ways of understanding I could not adequately describe or even come close to comprehend what was happening, but every pore of my being gave testimony to the legitimacy of this new experience of myself.

Chapter 6. Taking Hold

Meditation

It was some time after this that Sam re-introduced me to meditation. In previous years I had practiced various forms I had learned from books or acquaintances. Sam chided me on these misdirected efforts, indirectly, as he usually did when he wanted to suggest another way of looking at something.

"There are some people who sit in the lotus position and contemplate on their navel. Do you know what they get out of this? A stiff neck! Then there are those that try to empty their minds. Do you know what they accomplish? Nothing!" And he would laugh at his own joke.

"Before you begin, first take a shower. When you go for a job interview, you wash and put on your finest clothes. When you go before the Creator of the Universe, shouldn't you prepare yourself accordingly?" Then he taught me to concentrate on the Light and to focus it on my forehead, cleansing the mirror of the soul from accumulated "rust."

☙

At the start of my attempts at meditation, it was a kaleidoscope of colors, then images, and always some pesky stray thoughts intruding. For a period of weeks I thought I saw images of the history of humanity. Civilizations were parading past me in staccato precision, although the pictures never stayed in view long enough for me to truly grasp the details. Sometimes I imagined fantastic images but there was always the sense of falling, sinking, drifting deep within me. The "lower" I went, the harder it was to maintain the tenuous grip on consciousness and the more distracted I became by any minute changes in my physical or psychological environment. It was like balancing on a knife edge. Do I pay close attention to the visualization or revel in the feeling of peace? Do I maintain my composure or allow myself to drift off into mindlessness? Every step on this journey, the prayer, the meditation, was accompanied by self doubt. Was I really seeing images of civilizations with a new inner perception or were these the products of my imagination? Were my feelings of sinking and falling also self delusion? I shared these doubts with Sam. I didn't know what to expect in response. Would he chastise me for being impatient? Comfort me for my apprehension? Offer an explanation of what was happening to me?

"Excellent," he affirmed with a broad smile on his face. "I don't want you to believe anything I tell you. This path we are on, this is the straight way. Everything you learn, you learn for yourself. Then you will know and your doubts will..." His voice trailed off and he raised his hands slowly to the heavens.

I continued to meditate daily. This went on for weeks and the weeks became months. Meditation became a task, like a school assignment awaiting completion. I found it difficult to practice, and focused on the perceived obstacles to meditating. I set criteria for my meditation. It had to be quiet. It had to be dark. I had to be alone. Soon, there were more reasons not to do it as there were to do it. Didn't I have to be someplace else? Wasn't it essential to straighten up my room? Pay bills? Make a telephone call? Meditation was interesting and relaxing but I felt I wasn't getting anywhere or achieving anything. Sam was engaging me on different levels, intellectually, psychologically, philosophically, and now on what I hoped was a new and higher level. I grasped for signs of progress.

Then one day, I began to realize that a subtle change had occurred in the meditative process. The act of imagining or creating the visualization had become easier. The Light I thought I imagined in my visualization seemed to actually be there, in this ethereal space, a presence in front of me. I recognized the familiar feel of bathing in its primal power. Something of the peaceful intensity that I sometimes felt sitting with Sam was here, in this moment. I bathed in the Light, felt its peace and became refreshed.

Chapter 6. Taking Hold

Date

It was not unusual for me to complain to Sam if I did not have a date. I mean, if he was such a big shot, why couldn't he influence some hot babe to come my way? I was going through one of my routines when Sam was called away for a few moments. Someone pulled me aside and told me that Sam had just found out that his wife was in a terrible car accident in a foreign country. There were no details about the accident and Sam didn't know the extent of her injuries, if any. I felt like an absolute ass, but later, I marveled at Sam's composure, listening to my Saturday night hardships in the face of real life and death concerns. One day I asked him about this. "We are all in God's hands," was his only soft reply. He directed his gaze upward, his eyes half closing. A few days later I found out that his wife had been spared from serious injury.

The Real Deal

Almost a year had passed. My meetings with Sam were noticed by a few people at work but no one thought to question me. I never talked about it with anyone. I wouldn't know what to say. I learned a bit more about Sam, his family, his career, but this was not the focus of our visits. He was focused on me, my ideas, my experiences, my needs. He had a prescient quality of anticipating what was on my mind although I never bored of trying to trick him. He would ask "What's new?" or "What's on your mind today?" and I would often blabber some reasonably sounding calamity. "No, that's not it", he would say. If I failed to hit the correct nail, he would lapse into silence and close his eyes for what seemed like a long period of time, which was perhaps 30 seconds. He would take a deep drag on his pipe and then speak to my heart.

Sometimes the periods of silence would last several minutes and I would follow him into meditation. These periods were usually intense and marked by deep, enveloping peace. Sometimes these experiences would make me feel drowsy and I would drift off into contentment. After a while, he would say gently, "Ok, that's enough for now. If we stayed this way the whole day, who would do the work?"

I began to realize how much I had changed.
The things I thought I knew, about myself and my world view, I did not know. I had learned so much, but the essential learning was not rooted in facts or insights, although I could now speak with more authority on some issues. The "learning" was the fundamental change in who I was and the person I was becoming. I did not know what I needed to learn only that I was on a path that seemed to be taking me where I needed to be. This knowledge in itself was comforting.

Stew

I met Stew at work about a year after I met Sam. I was 23. It wasn't friendship at first sight: He was a clinical supervisor, always away from his desk, busy with many responsibilities; I was a research assistant, also busy, but engaged to a large extent in having to justify my time in the face of the next round of budget cuts. Stew was recently married. He was quiet and intense. Although our offices were close by there weren't many reasons for interaction between us. I don't remember how poetry became a topic of conversation, but after several months of chit chat, we both felt comfortable enough with each other to share some of our writings.

I was amazed to find in Stew a kindred spirit. His work was personal and revealing and he wrote about his closeness with nature and a yearning for meaning. I recognized in Stew the same spiritual longing that I had felt. I asked Sam if I could bring him over and he gave a little nod of the head and a smile.

Chapter 6. Taking Hold

I remember very little about what was said at that first meeting but I came to see Sam and the teaching presented in a different light. For one thing, this encounter lasted only about a half hour, and by the end of it, Stew was hooked. How did it take Stew so short a time to recognize Sam's specialness and to trust him? I came to realize that Sam would speak on topics or answer questions which Stew had not actually verbalized. As an observer, this seemed very strange, as if I was coming in on the middle of a conversation and did not hear the preceding remarks. But that wasn't the case. To Stew, the flow of conversation appeared natural. I saw Sam do this many times over the years and no one ever picked up on it. I also saw many more of my friends, Stew's friends and others take the same hesitant first steps to his office. All benefited from their meetings and some returned, attracted to the nectar of peace, inner harmony and contentment.

Reading: II

During one of our many conversations, I thought to ask Sam who his teachers were. Sam parried these questions. He asked if I would be interested in reading another slender tome. This was *The Alchemy of Happiness* by Al-Ghazzali. This led to *The Book of Strangers* by Ian Dallas, *Among the Dervishes* by Omar Burke, then *A Sufi Saint of the Twentieth Century* by Martin Lings. Later came *Tales of the Dervishes* by Idries Shah, *The Conference of the Birds* by Attar and a host of others.

Although Sam made me read some of these books over, and then over again, stating that I missed several key points, pieces of the puzzle were slowly coming together for me. I began to see the Teaching as a global network, a hierarchy of sorts, designed to preserve and pass on, to those that could use it, a special kind of knowledge which was the heritage of humanity. It was through these books that I became more familiar with the vocabulary and concepts of Sufis and Sufism, though throughout the many years of my association with Sam, he rarely used these words and never in the context of himself. Sam felt deep reverence for the historical Sufis. He felt that much was to be learned by reading about their lives and exploits. He would sometimes tell stories about them and made these ancient holy men come alive in my imagination.

I especially liked the books by Ghazzali and Dallas. The first, *The Alchemy of Happiness*, was a little gem and I have re-read it many times over the years. The second, *The Book of Strangers*, was a fictionalized tale that had elements of a present-day search for knowledge. It was written with a sense of mystery and excitement and appealed to my need to see spirituality in a modern context. A common thread to all of these books was the context of Islam. The Sufis operated within it and sometimes what appeared to be outside it, but never without it.

These books raised many questions for me, but Sam would not answer a question if he thought I knew the answer, if he thought I could easily find out the answer, if he thought the answer was not relevant to me or if the question was important for me to work through. On my own I asked fewer and fewer questions of Sam. It wasn't that I understood so much more, but in Sam's presence I no longer felt the need to ask. I gained an appreciation that what I was truly seeking was not the knowledge gained by academic study. The intellect can be a good launching point for inquiry, but some questions could not be answered in the same spirit in which they were asked.

Talking about the books or what was going on in my life was the context of our face-to-face meetings. But as I was to later understand, only a part of the "Teaching" was happening under my direct level of awareness. Sam noted that had I been born into a different culture, we wouldn't be speaking at all. Another time Sam said that much of the real teaching occurs when I'm sleeping! I found this impossible to understand and difficult to accept. So much

Chapter 6. Taking Hold

seemed to be happening in my most simple interactions with Sam. Sam once noted that music was a form of communication and through it you can connect to the person who created it. I felt this analogy was close to my experience with Sam. A melody was being created through our mutual experience and this melody was being made manifest into thin strands, joined by other strands into cords woven into a tapestry I could not yet see.

Doctor?

I did one of those jobs that were always on the chopping block in times of fiscal restraint: quality assurance, regulatory compliance, research and evaluation. And this head-hunting happened about twice a year. To some staff I produced no obvious patient-care service but only served administrative ends that they did not appreciate. Other staff saw me as a target because they had their own people that wanted to protect. My fate always seemed to rest upon the good wishes of back-door politicians. It was a source of constant anxiety to me although I never lost my job. One day, when I launched into yet another complaint routine, Sam asked me what I wanted to be when I when I was a small boy. I told him I didn't remember.

"You do remember," he insisted. You wanted to be a doctor. What happened?"

"This I don't remember," I pleaded. "Maybe it was my first biology course in college. Maybe I didn't have the grades to go to med school, maybe it was my interest in psychology. I really don't know...Why?"

"You were destined to be a doctor," he said.

"Huh?" was all I could manage.

"Yes, a doctor. You were supposed to be a doctor," he repeated.

"Then why didn't I?" I asked, unbelievingly.

"I don't know," he replied. "Maybe it's not too late."

"I didn't think it worked this way. Free choice and all," I said smartly.

"It doesn't, he said. "There are predilections, tendencies, and predispositions. Things don't always turn out exactly. After all, you did choose a career in the health field. But if being a doctor is what you want…"

"Wait a minute," I interrupted, "who said anything about me wanting to go to med school?"

"It isn't too late, you know, and if God wills, who knows what can happen?"

I had been disillusioned with my career as a psychology student but this suggestion both intrigued and frightened me. I was ready for a change in professional direction. Could this really be possible? I didn't think so. But Sam's endorsement gave this idea great credibility. The next day I plotted my course. I needed to go back to college to complete a year of organic chemistry and a year of physics. Four lab classes would equal two years with me working full time. I know I needed to ace the courses and explode on the aptitude tests for me to have any chance. But the best grades I could muster were B+. Coincidentally, I had begun to date a woman I secretly thought of as "La Belle Dame Sans Merci" and I could not concentrate on studying. My first MCAT science and math scores were only average. In subsequent tries, my science and math scores went up but not enough to raise anyone's eyebrows. Paradoxically, I scored a 760 on the subscale that taps general knowledge but my fund of general knowledge got worse with each test. So much for test reliability. I applied to med schools for two years, but by this time, had gained a senior management position with the hospital. I let it go. Perhaps this was not God's will.

Developmental Process

The Sufis were a remarkable people. I had come to know them through the stories of their many exploits and from

Chapter 6. Taking Hold

my deepening relationship with Sam whom I recognized as a latter day version. I had come to see my experiences and unfolding knowledge in the context of the Sufi tradition, although there were so many differences. A very important difference was that all had Muslim roots and were rooted in cultures based in the Middle East, Far East or Central Asia. Where did I fit in?

I viewed Sam's role, in part, as a Sufi Teacher and a bearer of the Sufi message to the West. There had been famous Sufis from many traditions. Sufis were in touch with the core of religious teachings. Their methods were consistent with the culture in which they operated. Their aim was the maintenance and transmission of Knowledge and the transformation of people, not the following of ritual or the spreading of doctrine. There was nothing linear or traditional, from the Western point of view, in their approach. I saw my experiences as consistent with the Sufi path and part of this process. I viewed much of what I was going through as preparatory: the scraping away and excision of unhelpful attitudes and obstacles to understanding. But the major field of play was life itself. Daily interactions provided the potential for growth and Sam was there to help me get out of life experiences what was there to benefit me. The growing perception of closeness to the Source was a blessing and was entirely out of my control.

Religion

I began to rethink the role of organized religion. Religion probably existed in its true form for only a short period. It was brought into existence to meet the needs of people at a given point of time, place and development. It required a living exemplar, a guiding force in touch with the essence of the ineffable. Something "living" still might remain at the core of their teachings, but it did not seem to be manifested in the way in which Judaism or Christianity expressed itself in the world. To me, what passed for religion seemed largely the fossilized remains of Truth.

Who could look at the current state of religion and imagine the initial projection, the time when it transformed people and brought them closer to God? The "religion" I was seeking seemed to bear as much resemblance to the sky as a painted picture. Who could imagine the expanse of the horizon, or the feeling of a breeze, if knowledge of these came only from the application of oils upon canvas? To find the source of "sky," one needed to look outside the painting. To find experience of Knowledge or Truth, I had to look outside the traditional formulations to the source of the current expression, the Sufis.

Islam and the Koran

Some commentators suggested that Sufis operated entirely within traditional Islam. Some stated that because they had penetrated to the depths of Truth, they were free to operate as they pleased. Yet others stated that their knowledge of the meaning of Islam was so deep, that even when it appeared that they operated outside of traditional bounds, they were always consistent with the higher Knowledge. All of this was way beyond my understanding and it presented a major problem. In order to truly understand the Sufis I felt I needed to penetrate the veil of Islam. And although I did not find a spiritual path in Judaism, I nevertheless was Jewish to my bones. I told Sam about my interest in Islam, thinking he would encourage me to explore this further, but to my surprise he urged me to go back to the Temple, that I would find new meaning for me there, in my own tradition. But I wouldn't hear of it. I was determined to try and gain a deeper understanding of Islam.

I picked up several translations of the Koran and was surprised to see so many differences. Some emphasized

Chapter 6. Taking Hold

the style or lyrical flow of the text; others seemed to sacrifice style in place of a more literal translation; some used the word "God," most used "Allah." I looked at side by side translations of the same section of text. Each seemed to give off a separate fragrance. Going by gut reaction alone, I settled on the Arberry edition. In my typical way of reading spiritual books, I scarfed it down quickly, eager to absorb any tidbits of information, only to read it slowly and more carefully the second time. I was impressed by the direct quality of the message. Unlike the stories of the Old and New Testaments, which were distant and related in the third person, I felt an immediate connection to the Koran, as if it was talking directly to me. I also had a push/pull attraction to the word "Allah." It was at once foreign and had a sense of "other," but it was also a word devoid of association as it did not conger old thoughts and prejudices of the Jewish or Christian presentation of God. I let myself experience my intuitive feel for the Koran without analyzing what I did not understand or criticizing what I did not like. To my surprise, I felt at home. When I told Sam about my explorations he recommended the translation by Yussuf Ali. I picked this up at the Islamic Center at 72nd and Riverside, and although I read many other versions, this has remained my prayer book ever since.

I met many practicing Muslims and felt much about them as I did practicing Jews and Christians. I did not share Muslim culture and knew little of their traditions, yet I recognized in reading the Koran something I did not recognize from reading other religious texts. Although I have read only English translations, and I know that these suffer in approximation, still I perceived the familiar scent of the Universal pouring forth from its pages. Holiness and meaning permeated the very pages and seemed independent of the words, which served as its vehicle. The Koran did not convert me to the religion of Islam, though in a fundamental way, at some point I felt myself to be Muslim, or at least one who aspires to surrender. In reading the Koran, I felt I found a key to the core of my Judaism. It was a door to understanding. One of my favorite Hebrew prayers begins: "You shall love your God with all your mind, with all your heart, with all your being." Which Muslim or any adherent to other religions could not claim these words as their own?

Mom

Moving out of the house was liberating for me but left my mother exposed. With no one to put her to bed when she passed out, put out her lit cigarettes when she fell asleep in bed, scour the house for full bottles, or throw away the empties, her drinking was bound to cross the threshold of my father's awareness. In any case, my concerns about what my father would know and when he would find out took a dramatic turn when the pattern of her drinking changed. It was no longer the late night binges when my father was out at the track with his friends, or the excesses at family gatherings in which my mother managed to embarrass a host of people except herself. Her drinking became less occasion-oriented and less clandestine. When she drank now she felt the freedom to express her fury, always directed at her husband who hadn't a clue what was going on. These were mostly inarticulate expressions of rage, easy for my father to dismiss as the rantings of a madwoman. In a strange, sad way, I thought her brave. She still had reserves of self respect buried beneath the years of psychological degradation. It didn't surprise me that my father was at a loss as to how to handle the emotional content of what my mother would say to him at these times but he knew the "situation" was quickly getting out of control. He began calling me at home, in a reversal of roles, pleading for my help. I, too, did not know what to do.

My father thought it would be a good idea for my mother to have a change of scenery . This translated into my taking my mother down to York, PA for a week's stay

Chapter 6. Taking Hold

at my brother and sister-in-law's house. He would pick her up the following week. While not quite half way, we always stopped at the Key Diner in Phillipsburg NJ for lunch. This trip was no exception. We eat our uneventful lunch, I asked for the check and my mother excused herself to go to the bathroom.

Five minutes. Ten minutes. Fifteen minutes and I was getting worried. No mom. I positioned myself near the bathroom door, ready to ask the next woman going there to look for my mother when mom staggered out, Drunk. She could hardly walk. I held her up and half carried her to the car. Her speech was unintelligible. I silently cursed myself for not checking her pocketbook, which was large enough to fit a small giraffe. I should have known better but at least she'd sleep it off on the way down to York.

I pulled away from the diner, wanting to put some distance between us and the staring eyes and reproachful comments. Back on the highway my heart stopped pounding and I slowly began to relax. Mom lay slumped in the passenger seat. I put on the radio and reached cruising speed About twenty minutes later I was singing to Neil Young when the passenger door flew open and mom was lunging out of her seat to throw herself out of the speeding car. Without so much as a thought I firmly gripped the steering wheel with my left hand, extended my right into a solid bar and smacked my mother across the chest as hard as I could, driving her into the car seat. Then again and again and again before she stopped struggling and settled into her seat. I pulled over to the shoulder and closed the car door. Mom slumped in her seat, head down, eyes vacant, whimpering.

We didn't talk much for the remainder of the trip and I was amazed how she was able to pull herself together in a semblance of respectability by the time we arrived. I knew Allen and Anita had already removed all their booze so the week would get off to a sober start. On Sunday when I was getting ready to drive back to NY mom approached me with a look of concern. "Michael." she whispered, "I lost my diamond wedding ring. I'm sure I don't have it." Two thoughts immediately came to mind. She lost it at the diner and my father will kill her. I told her I would return to the diner and ask, but I didn't believe it would be there. And it wasn't. This was years before "don't ask, don't tell" became a household phrase, but there was no need to tell my father and he was oblivious to the loss.

Weeks later I was leaving the hospital after work one day when I saw one of the patients from my ward, Charlotte, going on a pass. I asked Charlotte if she needed a lift and offered to take her to Westchester Square, a few blocks away. To say that Charlotte was huge doesn't do "huge" justice. I immediately began to regret my decision as Charlotte got into my little Corolla and tried to make herself comfortable. She was twice as big as the seat and the car literally rocked until she became settled. I was wondering how much it would cost me to replace the front shocks when we reached Westchester Square and Charlotte departed. And then I saw it. My mother's diamond ring was on the car floor having been dislodged by Charlotte's gyrations.

Back home from Pennsylvania. Mom continued to drink as before. She also denied that she had a problem and refused all offers of help. I explained the situation to Sam, told him I was calling in my chips and demanded that he intervene in some way.

"It doesn't happen this way," he said gravely, "you must act...and God willing, what needs to be done will happen through your intervention."

"But what am I supposed to do?" I implored.

"Act", he said decisively, "and may God bless you."

I left his office without having gained a sense of direction, feeling more lost and overcast than when I first came in. I did not have to wait for long before a direction became evident. A few days later my father called in the early evening and told me that my mother had tried to jump out

Chapter 6. Taking Hold

of the window. I hurried right over and when I arrived, was told an entirely different story from my mother, who while drunk, was still a more reliable reporter than my dad. Mom had thrown an iron at my father. She threw wildly and the iron had struck and broke a window. In the motion of swinging, she slipped and fell, bruising her hand and head on the window sill. Although I was glad mom didn't take that awful step, I realized that she could no longer be trusted to be left alone. I called the police and told them my father's version of what had happened.

The two officers that arrived will always live in my memory as models of sensitivity. They explained that Mom would have to be handcuffed and taken to the psychiatric ward of the local hospital. She didn't resist. All of the fight was out of her. My mother's face read of resignation and complete emptiness.

I dreaded the possibility of meeting someone my mother knew walking down the long hallway to the entrance of the building with the police leading the way. I have always felt that it was a great mercy from God that we met no one. In front of the house was a large paddy wagon. I got into the back with my mother and the door closed and left us in semi-darkness. We said nothing. The wagon had long ago lost its shocks and the ride was like a roller coaster. We did all we could to avoid being bounced off the walls. Our struggle for stability amidst our bouncing around lent a truly welcome mustard seed of humor to the situation.

At the hospital we had a long wait to see a foreign trained doctor who had not yet mastered his command of the English language. He was weary when he arrived and I could sense his frustration at trying to express himself clearly to us. He asked a battery of standard questions which I answered. My father was incapable of speech. The doctor did not want any elaboration or any background information about my mother. He did not care who she was or what the family dynamics were. He just wanted to know the immediate events that brought us to the hospital. With just the minimum of information, he was able to fill out form after form while we sat silently in the cramped admission office. My mother was sent to the psych ward.

Her sensorium cleared quickly without access to drink. The place really scared her. She was without all the creature comforts that she took for granted. Her routines, her shopping habits, her TV shows all were disrupted. She couldn't call her mother or her sister when she wanted. Most of all, she didn't want to be there with the crazy people. She attended AA groups in the hospital, and found enough support there to agree to attend them when discharged. She must have sworn to herself never to return to a place like this and she didn't. Within three weeks she was discharged. She attended AA meetings in the community for more than a year afterward and she was never drunk again.

One day after the emotion of these events died down, Sam asked me how my mother was. After telling him, Sam asked me to give money to charity.

"You received a gift," he said. "It is our way that when you receive such a gift, you return a gift."

Reverend Wells

One day I was sitting in my office working on something when Reverend Wells walked in. He was not tall, but a man of impressive stature, with a graying Afro and a voice any minister would be proud of. He could be commanding in a group or when the situation called for it or be soft and gentle when speaking one on one. He was widely respected by the few black professionals and greatly admired by the paraprofessionals. He could be provocative and persuasive and was not the favorite person of many high ranking white administrators. What was he doing walking into my office? I didn't have to wait long for an answer.

Chapter 6. Taking Hold

"Why is there so much turmoil in the world?" he demanded. He sat down in a chair opposite me, looked me squarely in the eye, but did not wait for my reply.

"Because," he went on, "they will not face, they will not embrace their anima. They reject this part of themselves and then project it onto others. What do you think of that?"

Somewhat stunned, partly by the force of his conviction, I replied hesitatingly, "I would have thought you might have said there is little faith in the world."

"Is that what you think?" came the retort.

With my "yes" a noticeable change came over him. He seemed puzzled and unsure, shook his head approvingly and said, "You and I will have to talk," and slowly started for the door.

"Reverend" I called out, "isn't it strange that you should speak of psychology and I speak of faith?"

"Yes," was all he said and walked out.

In the next few weeks he came prepared for battle. Armed with Jung's theories, John battered away at my faith. Psychology had become his religion. He was a skilled opponent with intelligence, quickness of thought and examples from every corner of human experience. His arguments all stemmed from the intellect and I recognized this line of attack, the one I would have used just a year or so ago. But by this time in my own development, I knew we were on different playing fields. John had sensed in me something that he had lost. He was looking for it in the only way he knew how. We both brought out the big guns: volumes of research, life experiences, voices from the masters, and when all else failed, we shouted.

Over the following weeks and months we became good friends. At heart, we shared personal goals but externally, our lives couldn't be any more different. He was an established adult with a wife and family, who had diverse experiences and jobs before coming to the church late in life. He was a leader in the hospital and a leader in the community, an advocate for the poor, for the disabled, for anyone that needed help.

At some point I introduced him to Sam, but to my surprise, John preferred talking with me. We remained confidants and looked like a very unlikely pair, until he stopped coming to work. No one would tell me what was going on, but when I did finally find out, I learned that John was dying from cancer. I went to his house for the first and last time and saw streams of people coming to say their last good-byes. When we were ushered into his bedroom, he was clearly exhausted and his family tried to shoo us out as soon as we came in. I didn't get a chance to speak with him but someone had told him that I was there. With his eyes half closed, I heard him say, "Tell Michael–I love that guy."

Intermediary

I brought many people to see Sam. Most found what they were looking for - a key to their own spirituality - in a single visit. I marveled at these people and the fact that it took me a year or so to learn what they seemed to absorb almost instantaneously. Many people kept in touch with Sam although almost none of them had the access to him as I did, working at the same agency. From time to time he'd say to me, "How's so and so?" and sometimes, without breaking stride, he would add, "When you speak to him, tell him..." Ninety-nine times out of a hundred these messages, which were often incomprehensible to me, had profound effects upon the recipient. Sometimes I bore messages back to Sam and became an intermediary of sorts. Sometimes people who aware of my closeness to him would ask me to ask questions for them. Some of the questions were personal, which caused me a bit of embarrassment, but sometimes questions were factual. In these cases, if I knew the answer, I would offer it.

Chapter 6. Taking Hold

After meeting one of my friends, Sam accompanied us to the door and as we were leaving he advised, "Stay close to Mike." The door closed. John and I just looked at each other. The message was clear to both of us. John was satisfied with this but I was both pleased and scared out of my wits.

I wasn't comfortable with my new role as intermediary. A part of me liked it and felt proud, but I knew it was undeserved. Thankfully, no one turned to me for advice. One day Sam asked me to gather the growing number of people who were coming to see him and hold a group meeting in my apartment where we could talk and pray. Sam had said that when one person prays, there is always an element of selfishness but when two or more people get together, it is for the love of God. He told me to ask each one to bring a dish so that no one person would be burdened. I didn't know what I was to do or expect and I was quite nervous as people started to arrive. But I didn't need to worry, things disintegrated quickly. As we sat around in a circle, someone I didn't know who came with a friend asked me, "What are you looking for?" I was taken aback. "Looking for?" I asked, somewhat incredulously. "Yes, Pam tells me that you are all looking for something I have found, and I have come here to share with you the glory that is Christ."

Within a few minutes most of the assembled group remembered important tasks they must attend to and scattered. The group was over. In the days that followed I thought about why I had felt so uncomfortable. The people had come because of the respect they had for Sam. They didn't come because of an internal need or because they wanted to be there. I resolved not to repeat this again.

Coffee Beans

Sam would offer his visitors whatever sweets he had lying about. One day he told me that he had one my favorites, chocolate covered espresso beans. This was no act of mystical mind reading, as he had seen me eat them plenty of times before. He gave me a small paper bag when I entered his office and I began munching away. When it was time for me to go, Sam asked me to look at the bag of beans. I had been eating them for over an hour and there were just as many beans in the bag as when I started. "Another gift," he smiled. While I was enjoying them, for God's sake, the supply would not diminish.

Mr. Haroun

One day Sam told me he wanted me to meet someone. He turned out to be Steve, who became a friend.

Steve was older than I was, undereducated and underemployed but smart. Steve marched to a different drum. He always had a different point of view –from everyone. It wasn't that he was ornery or difficult or testy. When you took the time to listen, he usually had a unique perspective: introspective, quiet, slow, sometimes moody and not psychologically oriented. I think he felt uncomfortable around people. Steve could fashion anything in wood with his hands. He knew more songs than anyone I ever met. I always thought Steve would be more at home at a farm in the Midwest, working with animals or things, away from people. What was he doing here so far away?

Steve was learning to read the Koran in Arabic and was referred to Sam by his teacher, Mr. Haroun. Steve had been a traveler on many spiritual paths, and after meeting Sam, soon became a new member in our loose confederation of spiritually minded misfits. One day Sam told me to visit Mr. Haroun.

"Why?"

"Because you will benefit from it." I tried to question him further, but he wouldn't say any more about it.

Steve arranged the visit and we went together in the early evening. I found out that Mr. Haroun was a high

Chapter 6. Taking Hold

ranking ambassador to the United Nations. On the rare occasions that Sam talked about Mr. Haroun, he referred to him with much respect, like a father or elder brother. I did not know what to expect of my visit, but I was not prepared for the encounter that followed.

We were greeted at the door by his wife and Steve did the talking. We were ushered into a small living room. It looked "hotel-like" with reasonably new furniture. It was pleasing to the eye, but devoid of taste. Only a few mementos from home were displayed. Time passed. His wife sat quietly in the living room while the children busied themselves with pre-dinner preparations. There was little small talk and I was feeling uncomfortable. It was clear from the wait that Mr. Haroun had not arrived from work. More time passed. I began to think that he had forgotten about our visit. It was now close to dinner time. He would be tired, hungry and not in the mood for Steve and me.

At last he came, a graying, middle-aged, olive complexioned gentleman who was conservatively dressed. He looked at us, and from the words that passed back quickly from he to his wife in some foreign tongue, I gathered that my assumptions were correct. He quickly washed up, and after a brief introduction, sat down in a comfortable chair, facing us. To my surprise his wife continued sitting where she was, and now the two were joined by their three children, who sat in respectful silence.

"What can I do for you?" he asked in a friendly, yet formal tone. I had no idea what to say. I felt unprepared for this moment. I started babbling, telling him that Sam had recommended that I come. He started shaking his head slowly with an unsmiling expression on his face. Steve, quiet as a mouse, was enjoying this.

"What do you want?" he asked pointedly.

If I was apprehensive before, I was reaching a new level of flutters. Some part of me decided to go for broke.

"I'm looking for truth," I blurted out.

The moment I said this I knew it was wrong. Even his placid children moved in their seats. Mr. Haroun apologized, but stated that he could not help me. In fact, he wondered why I came. We left soon after and I was in a total state of confusion.

When I saw Sam the next day, he grilled me on every aspect of the visit. He cringed when I told him about the "truth" part. I felt I had let him down.

"Not all Servants of God have been given permission to teach," Sam explained. "But there is a secret law among Servants that anyone who goes to one for help will not be turned away without a gift. Did you realize that he had given you a gift last night?" he asked.

I didn't want to say no, but it was clear from my blustering that I did not recognize the gift.

Steve and Sonia

One day, soon after I met him, Steve asked me to come home with him, have dinner and meet his wife ("don't worry, it's alright she won't care").

Sonia (She made up this name I was later to find out...What kind of people are these?) was not at home yet and Steve busied himself with something. I had ample opportunity to explore my new surroundings. They had very little money but every detail of their nouvelle post-hippy apartment was beautifully arranged, with care and with love. Green plants flourished; spices hung from kitchen corners; fresh fruit lay artfully arranged in plastic bowls. Deeply worn but richly colored rugs hugged the parquet floor. Art work, inexpensive and Far Eastern decorated the walls. I felt that I was only masquerading as a grownup while these two were real, whole, people that lived a bona fide life.

I knew I was in trouble the moment I saw Sonia. She was beautiful, captivating, charming and bright, witty and companionable, deliciously naive and unself-possessed.

Chapter 6. Taking Hold

Of course I didn't think all this the moment I saw her, this came thirty seconds later. The evening with them was a torture for me and I could not wait until my escape.

I was acutely aware of my thoughts and observations that evening and they scared me. What's worse is that all my fears were eventually realized. I saw Steve and Sonia's marriage in a stage of dissolution. I also realized that neither of them knew it. Steve's obliviousness to the world at large included his wife. His lack of competitiveness and motivation for something more and better was an irreconcilable divide between the two that would only deepen. Sonia's anger towards Steve was diffuse, subtle, unrecognized by both for what it was although acutely felt by both parties. I sat over dinner feeling guilty over my interest in Sonia, sensing her interest in my interest in her. I vowed never to see her again and spurned Steve's friendship for many months.

Years later, when they separated, Sonia and I had a brief affair and Steve and Sonia would later divorce. I think she might have left him anyway, but my emotional support and companionship may have been pivotal to her decision to leave him. I could not keep this from Sam and told him the truth. He told me that if I sinned against God, I could pray to God for his forgiveness. But if I hurt another human being, I had to turn to that person for forgiveness. Some time had passed and Sonia had long since found someone else whom she eventually married. In the meantime, Steve and I began reconciling our friendship through various intermediaries, both victims in a way, of the same cutie. I called him up and asked him to come over. He brought cookies, a good sign. We spoke and I asked him for his forgiveness. Although he said yes, it was many years before I could ask him that same question again, with sincerity.

—7—
Taking Off

Meditation

my eyes closed for the second time
all peace
all quiet
sinking, floating,
always the sense of movement ...towards...
I see the Lights that shine in universe of consciousness
and realize that I am seeing them
effortlessly I look at the vast expanse
thoughts flash across my mind: what has been created has always existed
it marks the stamp of its creator from the moment of its conception
this body, this soul and all that is, is part of this creation, its mysteries, its knowledge
each moment, a constant renewal
Image: the backyard of my childhood. Tall drab buildings, enclosing on all sides. I look at the doorway across the courtyard. A tree, tall, strong, imposing, spanning the height of the building. Many branches on top, small leaves. At first I thought it was dead. But no, it waits for the spring when nature will cause its leaves to thicken. A tree in hiding, maybe always hidden. It is not yet time.

Chapter 7. Taking Off

Passover

Passover was rolling around and I wanted to make my own Seder and invite the new people in my life. I wanted to keep the numbers manageable, but I didn't know if anyone at all would show up. I tossed the idea out to a few people telling them that I was thinking of doing this to gauge their interest. So I invited my friends, Sam and his wife and Reverend Wells and his wife. Almost everyone I talked to responded enthusiastically. I didn't think everyone would want to come and found myself with the pleasant problem of figuring out how to fit everyone in my small basement apartment. There was only one solution, I told my mother she was hosting it. She was delighted. It was a wonderful event with more non-Jews than Jews attending. I cherish the pictures I took of my guests being polite with the gefilte fish.

This humble beginning was to be the start of my own Seders. Over the years I discovered modern Hagadahs with contemporary wording and social themes. I began excerpting passages that interested me and added my own interpretations to such sections as the four sons and the search for the Afikomen (hidden).

Party

I don't know how I got reacquainted with Freddy. But we developed a new friendship that lasted a year or two until he got married and moved away. As sometimes happens between singles and newly married guys, we just drifted apart until we both stopped calling. While we were still friends he was planning a party and really wanted me to come. But I had a formal affair to go to and had to rent a tux, so I tried to beg off. He insisted, so I came over directly afterwards. I made quite a splash coming in so overly dressed and enjoyed the attention even if I was a bit embarrassed.

I met some of his friends and began talking to one woman who I learned was a new mother. In the course of conversation I said to her that she should continue to write. She had real talent and her writing would someday give pleasure to many people. This stopped her cold. How did I know she wrote? She told no one, not even her husband. When she was not grabbing a nap when her little one slept, she would write children's stories in a notebook that she squirreled away. No one had ever seen them. How did I know about it? Her questions were as surprising to me as they were to her. I knew the words came out of my mouth, but how did they get there? They were spoken with a sense of surety and without forethought.

Was this a lucky guess? If so, what were my clues? Did I pick up on some subtle communication? Even though she said she never discussed it? Or was this the process of a form of intuition operating at a different level that, up to this point, I was unaware of?

Sam often said factual things to me and my friends without the issue ever being discussed. I had grown familiar with his skill and when he and I were alone, took it for granted and no longer was surprised when it happened. I always enjoyed the shocked expressions from my friends when they encountered this for the first time. Now the situation was somewhat reversed. I didn't know if what had happened to me was the same process as Sam's, but the effect was the same. I told this young woman that her writing was a gift from God and to share her gift with others.

I began to think of myself as very special indeed and took this clairvoyance as further proof of my spiritual development. I was eager to try this new skill on others, and for days imagined I knew all sorts of other people's personal secrets. Reality sunk in when I realized that I didn't have any skill at all. What had happened, happened to the both of us. I could not read minds or spontaneously

Chapter 7. Taking Off

know things at will and began to see the dangers of having spiritual muscles without the temperament to control them.

Israel

One day, out of the blue, Sam told me that I had to go to Israel, that if I didn't go, something in my development could not go forward. It had to happen there. I was totally taken back. What did this mean? Was my development stuck? I was filled with apprehension and dread. Where was I to go? What was I to do? Was I going to fail to do what I had to do? Would I learn? Was I to meet anyone in particular? How would I recognize him? Sam would not answer my entreaties.

"Go" he said with a smile. He puffed on that pipe with that great cherry wood smell. "You'll see" he said softly.

So that summer, Marty and I packed our bags and went off for a three week vacation. When we arrived in Israel, I half expected one of the prophets to meet us at the airport with a chariot. When the terminal looked like a Hebraicized version of what I last saw 17 hours before, the magnitude of the task that I thought lay before me was great. I had not considered that I was not told to do any task at all, other than arrive. We picked up our rented car and drove into Tel Aviv. We went to the hotel that we booked for the first night, quickly unpacked, and went out to explore the old port city of Jaffa.

It was the end of the workday and the sun cast orange-lemon light that bounced off cars, shop windows and office facades. You could almost look at this sun, denuded of its midday powers. Its voice was silent, its presence was a muted strength. It suffused the corpuscles of space with deepening hues and shadows. Marty and I walked through the shards of light into the moist heat and dust of the crowded streets, blending with the mosaic of street life.

We surveyed our surroundings in English, Hebrew and Arabic, our first taste of the Israeli amalgam. Stores were going through the ritual of closing. Children and day laborers emptied garbage. Walkways were being swept with broken brooms. Shades were drawn closed. Anonymous people, in all manner of Western and traditional dress, moved with unknown purposes in familiar cacophony. We walked on until I noticed a pair of eyes-half-closed eyes sweeping from side to side, never raising to the plane of engagement. They reflected a reserved power and grace, a softness and restraint. They belonged to a figure completely shrouded in a swirl of black, flowing through the street as if through an invisible ether. Ankles, wrists and a slip of oval face. A dark, solitary jewel weaving her way through the street.

I don't remember what we said or how we decided, but we followed her. She never looked back but wended through side streets away from the crowds. We had no sense of why we were doing this. Another turn, then another, and she was gone. Only the fading light on white washed houses with glimpses of movement and the muffled sounds of life behind them remained.

We walked up the street in alertful silence. A child looked out from the security of an open window and followed us with an amused stare. A cricket jumped in our path and broke the eerie spell. A few steps up and to the right, a space appeared between two buildings. It was a large archway opening up into an inner court guarded by a small fence no more than two feet high. A few pairs of sandals were lined up just outside the fence against the wall. I felt that we had arrived at our mutual destination. But what were we to do?

I peered through the arch, looking for signs of welcome but found none. I wanted to go in but fear gripped my heart. I had visions of getting my ass kicked by a brood of athletic Arabic brethren eager to protect the virtues of

Chapter 7. Taking Off

their sister. I saw myself arrested for trespassing by non-English speaking police and hauled off to jail for the remainder of eternity.

We sucked up our courage, took off our sandals and slowly walked on the cool stones through the archway into the rectangular courtyard. It was much larger than what appeared from the street with several other arches around the perimeter, a small building to the left and a larger one to the right. A fountain was in the central portion of the communal space. We were in a mosque. My heightened senses were alive with danger and excitement. And then, as if on cue from a director of a movie wishing to inject a comedic interlude, a young man in Arab garb came out from some unnoticed doorway and began speaking to us in Arabic. We had no idea what he was saying and it didn't make a difference. He kept on talking, pausing at moments for us to respond. Using fractured English, that people sometimes use to speak to babies and the deaf, we tried to tell him that we could not speak his language, and asked him if he could please speak English. But he went right on, unperturbed. He began motioning us to the building on the right and we slowly moved in that direction. It was a large enclosed space with a floor covered with mats. The only thing that struck my attention about the room was a staircase leading nowhere. As we gazed about, taking in these new surroundings, someone else began talking to us. He picked up where the other left off.

He could have been 60 or even 80 years old by his gray hair and leathery face. But his movement had the agility and spirit of a younger man. His voice and gestures had an air of authority as he showed us around the mosque. My initial anxieties and agitation subsided as I found myself in a familiar inner landscape of peace and tranquility. After a few minutes we came to a corner where I saw the prayer niche. He made the traditional movements and postures of the Muslim at prayer and gestured for us to follow him. As we mimicked his motions, the old man raised his voice and began to pray and sing in Arabic. I felt he was praying for us, not only because we were unable to do so ourselves, but because, in some unknown way, we were benefiting from the act of hearing the prayer. As I sank down to the floor in the sitting position, I began to feel light-headed. I felt the power and awesome intensity of the prayer, riding on the couplets of the Imam's incomprehensible song. The glimpse of the presence of Love was overwhelming. I was in a state of humbleness. I was in submission, and yet still felt pulled by the urge to somehow go further.

As my knees touched the mat, and I bent my head forward to touch the ground, I felt my whole self sinking, as if the recesses of my being were tumbling into and through the prayer niche. The night sky emerged and bright lights of individual consciousnesses appeared on the horizon. This universe appeared vast yet invisible chords of light connected me to each conscious star. I recognized some friends and acquaintances and felt their presence with me in that very room. I sensed that I could reach back into time as well as touch the future.

I felt a tugging on my sleeve and I was roused back to the present. As we were walking towards the entranceway, the old man insisted that we give a donation for the upkeep of the mosque. We gave what little we had and made our way back in silence. Only later in the evening, when we spoke about what had happened, did we realize that we had the same experience. His voice had penetrated into our minds. We also realized that the old man spoke entirely in Arabic.

☙

We bought Sam a gift, a ceramic water jug. When we tried to give it to him upon our return, he became as angry as I had ever seen him.

"You western minds...Don't you realize that I, too, benefit from our relationship?" It was obvious that he was refusing to take it.

Chapter 7. Taking Off

"What am I supposed to do with it?" I implored.
"You'll know."

I took back the jug, and put it in a closet where it has remained unused for many years.

Guru Bawa

As a Village Voice reader/WBAI listener, I knew the dates of speaking engagements of every shaman, guru, pir, tribal elder and would-be money maker this side of the Hudson. Who were these guys? Did any of them know anything? Did any of them have anything to say to me? I asked Sam about them, from time to time, fully expecting him to try to talk me out of going to see them. I should have known better. Surprisingly, he told me to see anyone I liked! So I did. Feeling the self righteousness that only those on a holy mission can know, I spent many hours sitting in the back of ill-lit, crowded auditoriums, inhaling incense, listening to strange and beautiful bells, straining my eyes to get a glimpse of the solitary saint encircled by devotees.

I liked some more than others, thought some were deep thinkers, thought others were snake charmers, but even in the best of these public meetings, I always felt dissatisfied. I never felt the glimmer of a connection with the teaching or the man. I wondered whether this was my fault, that I wasn't developed enough in a spiritual way to sense the meaning and truth behind the tradition or teaching these men espoused.

I discussed my visits and impressions with Sam, who usually laughed at my descriptions. After one visit Sam said that a Servant of God never made references to himself, but only talked about God. Sam then surprised me and asked if I had plans to see Guru Bawa, the latest visitor to the New York metropolitan area. I said no, but silently made a note to myself to see him at the next speaking engagement.

Spiritual types are always late to their own audiences. Were they busy saving the world from destruction by emanating the power of goodness just at the moment when the crowd was gathered? Were they building up expectation and their own hype? Were they all constipated? These were my thoughts as I sat eager and hopeful.

Bawa was an ancient, shriveled man. He was dressed in a long robe and moved with the speed of the infirm. From far back in the room I could see his piercing dark eyes. I thought they were the only part of him that was alive. They had a power and intensity as they moved about the assembled. I could not sustain his gaze as he looked over the gathering and diverted my attention.

The interviewer, Lex Hixon, gave new meaning to the term "self-absorption" as he droned, heaping praises on the seated guru while telling the less fortunate all that he gained from his brief time with the master. Finally Bawa spoke. His voice crackled and chirped. Bawa spoke on a topic which I have completely forgotten, but before he did, he denied all the accolades which were heaped upon him. I remember only four of his words: "I am an ant," which were spoken with a sincerity that I have yet to fully comprehend. His words were directed towards my heart, and perhaps all the hearts in that dusty room. I knew that Bawa knew of his smallness. I knew that he lived in that smallness, that smallness was his state, that smallness gave him everything. For the briefest moment, I felt his "antness" and was devastated with its power.

These four words still live within me. They are Bawa's continuing gift.

Jan

When I wasn't going out with someone, which was often, I would be miserable. And if it was your lot in life to be counted among my intimate acquaintances, I would make you feel miserable too. I think one day Sam had enough of

Chapter 7. Taking Off

my whining. He stated in a matter of fact way that I already knew my wife and that she was a social worker. This shut me up fast and I quickly made a mental inventory of all the social workers I knew.

Since I happened to know a few, I started with the prettiest one and soon dated my way around to the B list. No wife there.

"So, I finally caught you in a mistake." I wasn't sure if this was a question or a statement, but when I saw Sam's expression of distaste I knew I was in for it.

"Think," he said. "You know her."

I had already gone through all my little black books for the past few years and completed my research in diligent fashion. I decided to drop the issue.

Months later, I was vacationing in Acapulco. I was coming out of the hotel elevator when a sexy, bikini-clad woman stepped in. The door closed and I stood there wondering where I had met her. Up in my hotel room later that day I figured out that we had met in college and even dated once, but she didn't look this good back then. I called the hotel operator and asked for her by name. If she was married and registered under her husband's name, so be it. The operator had no listing so I chalked it up to another one that got away and thought no more about her.

The next day, for a change of pace, I swam in the pool instead of the ocean. I lay down on a chaise and, uncharacteristically for me, took a mid day nap. Upon awaking, the bikini lady was lying down in the chair to my right. So I had no choice but to talk to her.

Jan hadn't planned to come to Acapulco, but a long dormant volcano had threatened the stability of Club Med in Guadeloupe and caused her sudden change in venue. Interesting, but it didn't click between us. I walked away thinking about the coincidences that brought us both to this hotel, neighbors around the pool. I asked myself, "Why not go back and give it another try?" What did I have to lose?

Three years later we were married. And yes, she is a social worker.

Getting Stuck on the Expressway

I had read, heard and experienced that help can come from the most unexpected sources. Skeptic that was, I still needed more proof. With the aid of hindsight I had come to see many unrelated instances of the shadow of the divine hand working in my daily life. But to see this "working" in the present tense, this "proof" eluded me.

As I was driving in rush hour on an elevated expressway, a three lane shoulderless excuse for a road replete with potholes, my car suddenly died. Not a unique experience, but for a person who had trouble finding the hood release mechanism, a potential nightmare. I sat there watching the cars whiz by me, hearing the cacophony of horns voice their displeasure, my anxiety rising. I knew I had to do something and I pictured myself standing over the engine block looking like I really knew something. Maybe I would fool the passers-by.

A car suddenly pulled up in front of me. A tall Hispanic man in overalls got out of his car with screwdrivers splayed in his hands. He came around to the driver's side window, told me he was a mechanic and asked if he could help. My reaction time could not have been faster and a wave of relief came over me. After performing what I thought could only have been a magical incantation under the hood he asked me to try starting the car a few times. My confidence was soaring, but nothing happened. He twiddled with the machinery. After a few more useless attempts, he told me he was sorry, that he could not help, and drove away saying that he would call AAA for me. I slumped back in my seat, thinking "God, You are playing a trick on me, right? What more do you have in store?"

No sooner did the mechanic pull away when another car pulled up in back of me. The driver got out and told me that he was off duty, but worked for an all news radio program. He called in my trouble to the helicopter that I now saw circling overhead. Using his car, he pushed my jalopy gently and, after a while, the engine came to life. He followed me to a gas station near my house and then left.

This event is certainly an unusual tale of kindness and good fortune in the big city. But to me, it had an additional significance: it was one of a series of faith-sustaining experiences that I began to see occurring or working in and around my life. I smiled to no one in particular and felt myself begin to loosen another of the grips that bound my understanding.

Am I walking with you, Jesus?

I often thought about the events that occurred in the Bible. Why did the prophets like Adam or Jonah disobey God? Didn't they, of all people, know better? If the best of humankind had moments of doubt, how was I supposed to think or act? I often imagined myself living in the time of Noah. Would I have believed his prophecy of doom, seeing this guy build a boat in the middle of nowhere? Would I have listened to Lot and abandoned the evil city of New York? Would I have recognized Jesus or been among the many that scorned him? And, if we are to believe the story as it is told, why did the people closest to him, abandon him in his time of greatest need?

I felt sure, as a matter of unthinking certitude, that had I been there, I never would have abandoned Jesus: the Jesus of love, Jesus my teacher. And then it occurred to me that I had a teacher, and my relationship to him, to the Teaching, to God, was, in some ways, parallel to that of the Jews in the time of Jesus and maybe similar to the path of many teaching relationships.

The question of loyalty and trust to the Teacher and the Teaching were new issues for me. I felt, in the core of my being, the undeniable truth of what I had experienced. I had found what I had been looking for: a path to Knowledge, a living tradition consistent with previous formulations and a human exemplar. Yet side by side with my new certainty of truth was a fear that I had been completely duped. What did I really know about Sam? Maybe he was a magician with powers to attract and hold people, as in trance. Maybe he was part of an elaborate cult that he would reveal when he felt the time was right. I know that he asked nothing from me or anyone I knew, but that may have been part of his subtle scheme and a key to his control.

I mentioned my current preoccupation, individually, to several of our throng as I tested my reactions against their sensibilities. My strange, short-lived game went something like this, "If Sam asked you to (name your own absurdity), no questions asked, would you do it?" The "winner," in my mind, was the person who asserted that he or she would do something that the other wouldn't. What made this contest of some interest was the fact that we were aware of the story of Moses who set out on a journey with his spiritual teacher. After three adventures, where seemingly destructive and hurtful events occurred, Moses had to part company but not without his teacher explaining the inner reasons for his seemingly inexplicable actions, something Moses knew nothing about.

The only absurdity I remember making up was my last one: "If Sam asked you, would you jump out of a 10th floor window?" While pondering the pros and cons of this one day the thought hit me that I was actually thinking about this! And I suddenly became aware of the feeling of discomfort which I had felt but did not acknowledge since embarking on this strange exercise. I realized that I had been willing to surrender parts of my self which were central to my own autonomy. How did I allow this to happen? Well, maybe I wouldn't do anything my teacher asked, but surely anything within reason?

But I couldn't do even this. On a seemingly superficial level, Sam had asked me to assist him once or twice on some research he was conducting. I made up all kinds of excuses to myself not to do this. Yes, I was in school and I had very little extra time, but these weren't the real reasons. Not only did I not help Sam, but on a basic level, I could not follow some of his simplest suggestions. Always, I followed those aspects of the teaching that were consonant with my personality or with my preconceptions of what I thought the teaching ought to look like. It was years before any of this became apparent to me.

Moving on

Over the years my visits to Sam became more infrequent and the tone of the visits changed as well. Sam was always happy to see me and was as cordial as ever, but he became less spontaneous and forthcoming about matters. I would sometimes leave his office wondering how he avoided certain topics or diverted the conversation. I felt that I was being weaned and that he wanted me to begin to find certain answers for myself. I once asked Sam about the ranks of the prophets and the saints. Who was more advanced and what did that mean? He stated that the prophets were in a different category entirely to themselves, but for all the others, there was only one criterion, love for God.

One of my grandmother's husbands was fond of asking me what I learned in school that day. My typical answer was: "Nothing. It's a waste of time."

"But look how much you have gained over the past year," he replied. "How did all these accumulated nothings add up to so much knowledge?"

As I looked back upon my post-Sam experiences, it is easy for me to see the continental shifts in personal growth but hard to relate specific events to changes in attitude. A fearful man-child became self accepting and trusting in the unfolding process of life. A life of rigid intellectualism gave way to faith. A diffuse yearning for mystical experience became transformed and focused towards submission to the One God.

I began to see people became attracted to a different me. I was positive, upbeat, and perhaps able to reflect some of the gift I had received through a more purified heart. I realized that it wasn't "me" that attracted people. It was the love that flowed through me. I had begun to think of my love for Sam in the same way. Sam was so many people to me: father, therapist, friend, and guide.

In the beginning, I was strengthened and sustained through Sam's love for God. He helped nurture long dormant possibilities in me and helped me find my true nature and purpose.

One day Sam told me that Idries Shah was the teacher of the age and I was to write to the Society for Sufi Studies in Palo Alto and tell them of my background and interest. This was it. I was being passed on to my next Teacher. I knew things wouldn't be the same between us and Sam sensed my sadness. "Our paths will cross again," he said with a broad smile. I didn't doubt him for an instant.

I felt a confusing mix of emotions. Shock, for I did not see this separation coming; pride, because with the separation was the unspoken acknowledgment that I was now able to carry out my studies on my own. Worst of all, abandonment. My easy access to Sam and the emotional bond I had with him, the checks on the excesses of my personality, was all to change. Although he never said the words, I felt them ringing in my ears: "You're an adult now. It's time to make it on your own." I wondered for an instant if I had done something wrong, if I was being kicked out of the spiritual path, but Sam said no. I also felt afraid that I might fail, afraid I would get lost in my own misunderstandings, afraid I would be sidetracked by spiritual sideshows and not recognize what would be best for me, afraid that pride and egotism might hinder my progress. I wanted to ask a thousand questions: Is there a natural

Chapter 7. Taking Off

course of spiritual development? What stage or station did I occupy? Would I ever become a Sufi? What did I need to do next? But Sam already told me.

I wrote to the Society for Sufi Studies, told them briefly about myself and that Sam had recommended me. I checked my mail box every day for a response. A few weeks later, a thin letter arrived. I don't know what I had expected, but I immediately felt that I was back in college and I had been rejected by all the grad schools I had applied to. So thin. What could they possibly have said? Sorry, buddy, we have telepathically scanned your progress and we regret to tell you that you have to wait another lifetime. Contact us then. Or was I going to be contacted by my local enfranchised Sufi teacher? Was I to join an existing study group? Would they look down on me as a newbie? My heart was pounding. I opened the letter and was so excited I couldn't read it. When I calmed myself down I wasn't ready for what it said. There was a list of about 20 books written by Idries Shah. I was to study them, and after I did, I could write back if I wished. Now, I had some interesting experiences and had a bona fide Sufi Teacher in the flesh guiding me for a period of years. What I didn't need at this point was books. I was furious. I was embarrassed. Did I accomplish nothing? Who were these people?

Days passed. I began to think more rationally, even optimistically. First, I hadn't been rejected, and second, they had given me a course of study. I called Sam to tell him about my reactions. He just laughed and said "Read the books!" So I bought them all and tried to gobble them down as quickly as I could speed read them. But I couldn't. The material did not lend itself to a quick read. There was much nutrition here in a form I was not accustomed to. If I was to do this seriously, I had to slow down and get from this material what I could.

Reading and learning from teaching stories took some getting used to. I had to learn to approach them differently. One way was to recognize the elements of the story as representing different states of mind. Some stories I liked and others I didn't. I wanted to look at them closely and understand why some appealed to me and others didn't. Others I would hold in my mind as if they were a tonic to some unknown psychic malady.

Time passed and the day to day repetitiveness of my life took an inexorable toll on my unrealistic expectations I stopped expecting. Idries Shah was not going to appear on my doorstep and personally teach me. I went back to the books and re-read them.

And then the "pops" started to happen. I called them pops because I would be speaking with someone and then a story from one of the books would suddenly pop up in my mind. I would become aware that I was re-enacting a theme or a relationship that appeared in one of the stories. I remember being pressured by a high ranking government official at work to take a certain course of action that I wasn't comfortable with. Although the person was clearly in a position of authority, the issue was mine to deal with and not under his jurisdiction. How to extricate myself from this situation and save face at the same time? Without a word of introduction, I began telling the story from one of Idries Shah's books about the army general who became separated from his troops at the time of war and rode into a village on horseback. He starts ordering the people about. "You, over there, water my horse, you – get me something to eat," and so on. The villagers gathered about and started questioning the soldier. "And what would happen if we fail to carry out these orders?" Well, I'll call the Captain and he'll call the Sergeant and the Sergeant will line you up by the wall and shoot you." "Well," replied the villagers, "had the Sergeant been here, a man of real power, that would have been something!" No more was asked of me.

Even more frequently than the remembrance of the teaching stories, conversations with Sam which I had long forgotten would crystallize in my mind at appropriate moments as if drawn from a reservoir of teaching inside me.

Chapter 7. Taking Off

These pop-ups were very much like the teaching memories of Kwai Chang Caine on the TV show, *Kung-Fu*. Life was proving to be stranger than fiction. These pop-up experiences gave me confidence in myself. My spiritual side was growing and my learning was continuing.

Months afterwards, a friend of mine, who knew me for over twenty years, said in passing that I was the most spiritual person she knew. This upset me a great deal. I didn't know what she meant and didn't want to know. I didn't think of myself as spiritual. I was just me. I was no teacher, no role model, no one to look up to. What could she be thinking? I let this sit with me for a few days until I allowed myself to think dispassionately on our friendship. I had been a friend, someone she could turn to for emotional support and guidance. When she was down, she leaned on my faith for support. My beliefs had become central to who I was, and this had become important to her.

In the beginning of my spiritual journey, my experiences were things that happened to me. By what strange alchemy had they become me?

Epilogue

I've come downstairs from my bedroom to the kitchen, drawn by the smell of freshly brewed coffee. The carafe sits on the counter full of the dark luxurious liquid. Next to it is the blender, a container of non-fat plain yogurt and fresh berries ready for mixing. Yesterday's dinner plates lay piled in the sink. The Sunday Times covers the kitchen table. The magazine section is already opened to the crossword puzzle and a pen sits on top.

Do I need to see my beloved to know of her presence?

About the Author

Along with a lifelong involvement in Sufi studies, Michael has worked in both New York and New Jersey state mental health systems primarily in the areas of quality management, corporate compliance, administration and patient safety. He is married to Jan Alscher, a psychiatric social worker and has two grown sons, Noah and Nathaniel. Currently, Michael is a college teacher in psychology and a volunteer with the Institute for the Study of Human Knowledge.

Notes

This book could never have happened if not for the continuing support of my two brothers in this journey, Stewart Bitkoff and Martin Barth. Special thanks to my wife Jan for all her help and support. Important readers along the way who offered ideas and encouragement include Joel Silbert, David Paquoit and Asheka Troberg. Jennine Cabrera offered advice, encouragement, editing and helped me to clarify my thoughts. If parts of this manuscript are clear and coherent, it is due to her efforts.

NO PEOPLE WERE HARMED IN THE MAKING OF THIS BOOK. Obviously, this book is, in part, a collection of memories. I may not have gotten all the facts right and I am truly sorry if I unintentionally misrepresented any event or personal interaction.

A few closing words about Sam. Many years have passed from the end of my story to the present. At first I continued to see Sam, though infrequently; in recent years, only an occasional phone call. There are no words that can express the bond forged between teacher and student. The love and the trust are closer than that of mother and child. To Sam I offer gratitude and a humble heart.

www.ingramcontent.com/pod-product-compliance
Lightning Source LLC
Chambersburg PA
CBHW031641040426
42453CB00006B/174